M000103040

# The Buffy Chronicles

## The Unofficial Companion to

### *BUFFY THE VAMPIRE SLAYER*

———

This book has not been prepared, licensed, endorsed,

or in any way authorized by any entity that created or produced

*Buffy the Vampire Slayer.*

ALSO BY N. E. GENGE

*The Unofficial* X-Files *Companion*

*The Unofficial* X-Files *Companion II*

*The Unofficial* X-Files *Companion III*

*The* X-Files *Lexicon*

*Millennium: The Unofficial Companion* (vol. 1)

*Millennium: The Unofficial Companion* (vol. 2)

# The Buffy Chronicles

The Unofficial
Companion to
*BUFFY*
*THE VAMPIRE SLAYER*

N. E. GENGE

Three Rivers Press
New York

Copyright © 1998 by N. E. Genge

All rights reserved. No part of this book may be reproduced or transmitted in any form or by any means, electronic or mechanical, including photocopying, recording, or by any information storage and retrieval system, without permission in writing from the publisher.

Published by Three Rivers Press, a division of Crown Publishers, Inc., 201 East 50th Street, New York, New York 10022. Member of the Crown Publishing Group.

Random House, Inc. New York, Toronto, London, Sydney, Auckland
www.randomhouse.com

THREE RIVERS PRESS and colophon are trademarks of Crown Publishers, Inc.

Printed in the United States of America

Design by Kay Schuckhart/Blond on Pond

Library of Congress Cataloging-in-Publication Data
Genge, Ngaire.
    The Buffy chronicles : the unofficial companion to Buffy the
vampire slayer / N.E. Genge. — 1st pbk. ed.
    Includes bibliographical references.
    1. Buffy the vampire slayer (Television program).   I. Title.
PN1992.77.B84G46      1998
791.45'72—dc21                                              98–28785

ISBN 0-609-80342-5

10 9 8 7 6 5 4 3 2 1

First Edition

*For Peter and Michael:*
*Thank you.*
*I love you.*

# Contents

ACKNOWLEDGMENTS . . . . . . . . . . . . . . . . . . . . . . . . . . . . . . . . . . . . . . . . . .xi
INTRODUCTION . . . . . . . . . . . . . . . . . . . . . . . . . . . . . . . . . . . . . . . . . . . . . .xiii

## Season One

"Welcome to the Hellmouth" (Part 1)/"The Harvest" (Part 2) . . . . . . . . . . . . . . . . . . . .3
    Building the Buffyverse . . . . . . . . . . . . . . . . . . . . . . . . . . . . . . . . . . . . .4

"The Witch" . . . . . . . . . . . . . . . . . . . . . . . . . . . . . . . . . . . . . . . . . . . . . . . . .11
    The Finer Points of Witch Detection . . . . . . . . . . . . . . . . . . . . . . . . . . . . .11

"Teacher's Pet" . . . . . . . . . . . . . . . . . . . . . . . . . . . . . . . . . . . . . . . . . . . . . . .19
    Virgins: The Endangered Species . . . . . . . . . . . . . . . . . . . . . . . . . . . . . . .19

"Never Kill a Boy on the First Date" . . . . . . . . . . . . . . . . . . . . . . . . . . . . . . . . .27
    In the Club: The Case for Secret Identities . . . . . . . . . . . . . . . . . . . . . . . .27

"The Pack" . . . . . . . . . . . . . . . . . . . . . . . . . . . . . . . . . . . . . . . . . . . . . . . . .33
    It's Amazing What You Can Find in Books These Days . . . . . . . . . . . . . . . .33

"Angel" . . . . . . . . . . . . . . . . . . . . . . . . . . . . . . . . . . . . . . . . . . . . . . . . . . . .41
    Whither from Here? . . . . . . . . . . . . . . . . . . . . . . . . . . . . . . . . . . . . . . .41

"I, Robot—You, Jane" . . . . . . . . . . . . . . . . . . . . . . . . . . . . . . . . . . . . . . . . . .49
    Away from the Cauldron and on to the Internet . . . . . . . . . . . . . . . . . . . .49

"The Puppet Show" . . . . . . . . . . . . . . . . . . . . . . . . . . . . . . . . . . . . . . . . . . . .57
    Hunting Demons . . . . . . . . . . . . . . . . . . . . . . . . . . . . . . . . . . . . . . . . .57

"Nightmares" . . . . . . . . . . . . . . . . . . . . . . . . . . . . . . . . . . . . . . . . . . . . . . . . . . . . . . .65
    I Spy with My Sleeping Eye . . . . . . . . . . . . . . . . . . . . . . . . . . . . . . . . . . . . . .65

"Invisible Girl," a.k.a. "Out of Sight, Out of Mind" . . . . . . . . . . . . . . . . . . . . .73
    All Hail the Queen of the May! . . . . . . . . . . . . . . . . . . . . . . . . . . . . . . . . . .73

"Prophecy Girl" . . . . . . . . . . . . . . . . . . . . . . . . . . . . . . . . . . . . . . . . . . . . . . . . . . . . .79
    The Good Guys . . . . . . . . . . . . . . . . . . . . . . . . . . . . . . . . . . . . . . . . . . . . . . . .79

## Season Two

"When She Was Bad" . . . . . . . . . . . . . . . . . . . . . . . . . . . . . . . . . . . . . . . . . . . . . . . .93
    The Bad Guys . . . . . . . . . . . . . . . . . . . . . . . . . . . . . . . . . . . . . . . . . . . . . . . . .93

"Some Assembly Required" . . . . . . . . . . . . . . . . . . . . . . . . . . . . . . . . . . . . . . . . . .103
    There's Gold in Them There Graves! . . . . . . . . . . . . . . . . . . . . . . . . . . . . .103

"School Hard" . . . . . . . . . . . . . . . . . . . . . . . . . . . . . . . . . . . . . . . . . . . . . . . . . . . . .109
    Daddy, Dearest . . . . . . . . . . . . . . . . . . . . . . . . . . . . . . . . . . . . . . . . . . . . . . .109

"Inca Mummy Girl" . . . . . . . . . . . . . . . . . . . . . . . . . . . . . . . . . . . . . . . . . . . . . . . .117
    You Say Ampata, I Say Ampato . . . . . . . . . . . . . . . . . . . . . . . . . . . . . . . . .117

"Reptile Boy" . . . . . . . . . . . . . . . . . . . . . . . . . . . . . . . . . . . . . . . . . . . . . . . . . . . . . .123
    Hazing: The Real Ritual . . . . . . . . . . . . . . . . . . . . . . . . . . . . . . . . . . . . . . .123

"Halloween" . . . . . . . . . . . . . . . . . . . . . . . . . . . . . . . . . . . . . . . . . . . . . . . . . . . . . .129
    As American as . . . Halloween? . . . . . . . . . . . . . . . . . . . . . . . . . . . . . . . . .129

"Lie to Me" . . . . . . . . . . . . . . . . . . . . . . . . . . . . . . . . . . . . . . . . . . . . . . . . . . . . . . .137
    Vampire Wanna-Be's . . . . . . . . . . . . . . . . . . . . . . . . . . . . . . . . . . . . . . . . . .137

"The Dark Age" . . . . . . . . . . . . . . . . . . . . . . . . . . . . . . . . . . . . . . . . . . . . . . . . . . .143
    When It's Hard to Get Your Z's . . . . . . . . . . . . . . . . . . . . . . . . . . . . . . . . .143

"What's My Line?" (Parts 1 and 2) . . . . . . . . . . . . . . . . . . . . . . . . . . . . . . . . . . . .149
    When I Grow Up, I Wanna Be . . . . . . . . . . . . . . . . . . . . . . . . . . . . . . . . . .149

"Ted" . . . . . . . . . . . . . . . . . . . . . . . . . . . . . . . . . . . . . . . . . . . . . . . . . . .159
   The Death Toll . . . . . . . . . . . . . . . . . . . . . . . . . . . . . . . . . . . . . . . . .159

"Bad Eggs" . . . . . . . . . . . . . . . . . . . . . . . . . . . . . . . . . . . . . . . . . . . . . .175
   A Tisket, a Tasket, a Faux-Baby Basket . . . . . . . . . . . . . . . . . . . .175

"Surprise" (Part 1)/"Innocence" (Part 2) . . . . . . . . . . . . . . . . . . . .183
   Your Intentions, How Honorable? . . . . . . . . . . . . . . . . . . . . . . . .183

"Phases" . . . . . . . . . . . . . . . . . . . . . . . . . . . . . . . . . . . . . . . . . . . . . . . .193
   What's a Little Howling Between Friends? . . . . . . . . . . . . . . . . . .193

"Bewitched, Bothered, and Bewildered" . . . . . . . . . . . . . . . . . . . . .203
   Charmed to Meet You . . . . . . . . . . . . . . . . . . . . . . . . . . . . . . . . . .203

"Passion" . . . . . . . . . . . . . . . . . . . . . . . . . . . . . . . . . . . . . . . . . . . . . . .211
   I Fall to Pieces . . . . . . . . . . . . . . . . . . . . . . . . . . . . . . . . . . . . . . . .211

"Killed by Death" . . . . . . . . . . . . . . . . . . . . . . . . . . . . . . . . . . . . . . .217
   Introducing Mr. Death . . . . . . . . . . . . . . . . . . . . . . . . . . . . . . . . .217

"I Only Have Eyes for You" . . . . . . . . . . . . . . . . . . . . . . . . . . . . . . .225
   What in Hell(mouth) *Was* That?! . . . . . . . . . . . . . . . . . . . . . . . .225

"Go Fish" . . . . . . . . . . . . . . . . . . . . . . . . . . . . . . . . . . . . . . . . . . . . . .233
   Who's Afraid of the Water? . . . . . . . . . . . . . . . . . . . . . . . . . . . . . .233

"Becoming" (Part 1)/"The Whistler" (Part 2) . . . . . . . . . . . . . . . . .241
   Surviving the Longest Months . . . . . . . . . . . . . . . . . . . . . . . . . . .241

Trivia Scorecard . . . . . . . . . . . . . . . . . . . . . . . . . . . . . . . . . . . . . . . .255

Photograph Credits . . . . . . . . . . . . . . . . . . . . . . . . . . . . . . . . . . . . . .256

# Acknowledgments

My favorite part!

Though writing is often a lonely occupation, this project was made unendingly delightful and rewarding by the generous assistance of the many people who've helped bring this book together. My thanks to:

Paul Sapper, friend and colleague, for arguing loudly and well.

Dan, John, and Steve, for coming up with oddities on short notice. One day, I *am* going to take pictures of everything in your closets!

The many men and women named in the articles that follow, all of whom unselfishly shared their experiences and knowledge, not to mention their patience and good humor, with a jack-of-all-trades who is master of none. Unfortunately, you were *all* so interesting that I still can't settle on any one field, but I will be back!

The staff at the Captain William Jackman Memorial Hospital who allowed two researchers, with cameras, to wander through their morgue and other strange corners.

Ling Lucas, an outstanding agent who is also a wonderful friend.

Ellen van Wees, who frequently provides more assistance than she realizes.

Lorna Sainsbury, appreciated as much for her cheerful smile as for her deft hand on the receipts and the shutter.

John Sainsbury, who tracks the weirdness, locates the lost, and manages to uncover the real oddities.

And Peter and Michael, though thanks don't begin to cover my gratitude for all the times your schedules have come second to mine without complaint, for your support, your seemingly endless kindnesses, your laughter, and your love. Thank you.

# Introduction

Not everyone gets a second chance.

In Hollywood, you're lucky to get a *first* chance.

Even if your name is Joss Whedon and you've just walked away with an Oscar for *Toy Story*, and even if everyone knows it was your sure touch that kept *Waterworld* afloat and *Speed* on track, the chance to return to a project and, excuse the pun, completely revamp it comes to only a handful of writers. Getting to do it as writer *and* director *and* as the general creative god now known as "series creator," is, well, practically unheard of!

Even with a string of incredible writing credits, Whedon might have been stuck with nothing more than the original *Buffy the Vampire Slayer* movie, with all of its irksome shortcomings that kept him coming back to the idea of a series for six years after the movie was put in the can, if a unique period in modern television history hadn't kicked in fortuitously.

A blockbuster hit called *The X-Files* was making speculative fiction cool again, and every network wanted its own supernatural drama. Dozens of shows had already failed: *Nowhere Man*, *Dark Skies*, *Space: Above and Beyond*, *The Visitor*, all critical hits, all canceled. They simply failed to draw in an audience. *Buffy the Vampire Slayer*, however, already had an audience. Though never living up to Whedon's hopes, the original movie, like such diverse films as *The Rocky Horror Picture Show*, which still defies categorization, and *Somewhere in Time*, a time-traveling romance, quickly reached the elite category of "cult mainstay." Years after its release, a recognizable section of film fans continued to discuss *Buffy the Vampire Slayer*, to watch it when it was rereleased in video, and to want more!

"Big screen to little screen," and vice versa, was huge when Whedon got serious about creating a series more true to his first vision of Buffy. *Star Trek* had made a regular business of shuffling its actors back and forth between film and television. *The Brady Bunch*, *The Flintstones*, *The Saint*, and *Mission Impossible* carried waves of television viewers into the theaters. Big-screen concepts, with the rapid improvements in technical quality and the line between film and television actors blurring, were also coming to weekly television: *Silence of the Lambs* fans could tune in to *Profiler* or *Millennium* while waiting hopefully for *Lambs 2*. Adaptation to and from film, television, plays, and books was the concept of the moment.

The youth horror market, a genre apparently unknown before the advent of *Goosebumps* and *Crypt Tales*, was booming. Through careful filming and creative staging, *Buffy the Vampire Slayer* could entertain not only the college-age students who would see their younger selves reflected in the main characters, the older viewers who had hit the theaters when the film first played, and the more mature viewers who could wax nostalgic while being scared on a weekly basis, they could draw deeply on that expanding youth market!

The TV market's rapidly changing profile also made "marginal" projects more attractive. There were more people to watch TV, but smaller networks were taking a share of the viewers, and the viewers were being actively wooed by dozens of specialty networks. The Big Three networks might not back an unusual offering, but the new networks, the swiftly growing minis, were desperate for quality projects; "name-brand" recognition of *Buffy* the movie could only make the idea of *Buffy* the series that much more attractive. For WB Television and *Buffy the Vampire Slayer,* the situation was ideal. The Frog got a series from a popular writer, writing for their market; *Buffy the Vampire Slayer* found a home with a network that was willing to let the series grow and build its own new following to complement the Buffy film's existing fan base. While NBC, ABC, and CBS were dumping a third of their new series after only *four* episodes, WB Television and Fox were determined to go the distance on the first half-season of episodes. It payed off big time. The rating numbers were creeping up and, better yet, all the buzz—and there was plenty of it—was good!

WB Television was happy, the fans were happy, and finally, Joss Whedon was happy.

The *Buffy* series, while keeping all the delightfully campy dialogue, the action, and the humor, finally became the true horror show Whedon envisioned when he first penned the original script to the 1992 movie. Describing his role during the movie's filming, in a recent interview, Joss Whedon's most telling statement perfectly illuminates the differences between then and now. "Making a movie to me is like buying a lotto ticket. The writer is not that important. In *Buffy* the movie, the director took an action/horror/comedy script and went only with the comedy. In the TV show, we are keeping to the original formula. We take our horror genre seriously." And now, as the creative executive on *BTVS,* he's free to do just that.

The changes are obvious.

In "Welcome to the Hellmouth," the series premiere, which incidentally was only a few minutes shy of its cinematic predecessor's running time, it's the horrific side of the tale that stands out. The Master's vile countenance rising from a seemingly endless pool of blood, the harsh grunge appearance of his Vessel, a creepy vampiric conduit who channeled soul energy back to his Master from Sunnydale's buff young teens, the serious scream value incorporated into dimly lit scenes, which gave the viewer's imagination more play than anything to come from the brightly shot original. We were still laughing at lines like Cordelia's classic: "Oh, puh-lease! I don't mean to interrupt your downward mobility, but I just wanted to tell you that you won't be meeting Coach Foster, the woman with the chest hair, because gym was canceled due to the *extreme* dead guy in the locker." But, this time, we checked under our beds, too.

Over the following episodes, Joss Whedon and his writing staff continued to artfully blend classic monsters with teen angst, making the old new, and making it creepier as it was enacted through characters from our own experiences. For the true cult fan, watching *Buffy the Vampire Slayer* is a trip through the very best horror has to offer, a trip this book attempts to expand on because, as dramatically adept as this program already is on its own, it absolutely shines when seen within the context of its own genre.

# Season One

A Slayer and her Slayerettes.

# "Welcome to the Hellmouth" [Part 1]/ "The Harvest" [Part 2]

the short version

**Part 1:** Buffy, ex-cheerleader and fashion critic, has arrived in Sunnydale to start over. No more slaying vampires during study period. No more demolition of school property, no more Watchers judging her slaying techniques, right? Wrong. Dead wrong. Only two days at her new school, and she's already tripping over corpses sporting bite marks instead of hickeys, and ducking a librarian determined to pick up where her last Watcher left off. Before the second night is out, she's alienated the coolest girl at school and blown the Slayer secret identity clause. As she tries to explain the parameters of vampire slaying to an astonished Willow and Xander, a Master Vampire plots more trouble for her.

**Part 2:** Sunnydale is crawling with vampires who await a mystical convergence called the Harvest, which is due to descend upon the unsuspecting people of Sunnydale at any moment— unless Buffy and company can sidetrack the Master. Of course, the Master has his own team in the field. Darla, Luke, and the newly made Jesse are only the beginning. Slayer strength just isn't enough when the Master turns Luke into a Vessel designed to siphon energy back through the mystical cage holding him, thus allowing him to attempt to escape. The suckfest is poised to begin, and Buffy will need all the information Willow, Xander, and Giles can throw her way if she's to survive.

the longer look

## SLAYER-IN-TRAINING TRIVIA

### QUESTIONS

1. **Who was born April 14, 1977?**

   A. Alyson Hannigan
   B. Sarah Michelle Gellar
   C. Charisma Carpenter
   D. Anthony Stewart Head

2. **Who portrayed Buffy in the original *Buffy the Vampire Slayer* film?**

   A. Kristy Swanson
   B. Sarah Michelle Gellar
   C. Marina Sirtis
   D. Gillian Anderson

3. **Who is Sarah Michelle Gellar's stunt double?**

   A. Bianca Lawson
   B. Mary Lou Retton
   C. Marti Noxon
   D. Sophia Crawford

4. **Who performs the theme song for the *Buffy the Vampire Slayer* series?**

   A. Marilyn Manson
   B. Def Leppard
   C. Alice Cooper
   D. Nerf Herder

# Building the Buffyverse

Tackling the accumulated myth, folklore, and Hollywood hype that's evolved into modern vampire mythology is, for writers, only slightly less hazardous than taking on the nightstalkers themselves without the handy-dandy vampire kit that's been part of the vampire slayer's key accessories since Abe Van Helsing decided to track down Dracula. In creating the backdrop for the original *Buffy the Vampire Slayer* movie, every artistic choice had to be weighed against a mass of "facts" that added up to the standardized vampire—without becoming the stodgy stuff more likely to bore viewers to death than scare them silly. Then there were the technical considerations. Flying vamps, in addition to simply being cooler than earthbound ones, open up nifty opportunities for creative scene framing, but leave the behind-the-scenes bean counters groaning over the additional costs of extra cameras, booms, and crew.

By the time *Buffy* came to the small screen, creating an environment both traditional and original was further complicated by a need to remain consistent with the movie and the vampire genre, while still leaving room for audiences to discover new twists and for writers to craft dramatic episodes week after week. The show's creators also had to keep in mind that a television budget wasn't going to allow for an FX-fest every full moon, a serious consideration for a program that might, at first glance, appear to be something of a lightweight in the character department. Whatever set of rules eventually emerged had to satisfy both the "Vampires don't do that!" crowd and the near-obsessive *Buffy* aficionado murmuring in the background, "But he never flew before. . . ."

As it happens, Buffyverse vamps definitely do fly. Whether you call the swirling over Cordelia's head in the parking lot low-budget or simply understated, it fixed flight ability forever within the repertoire of Sunnydale vampires. For the string of writers contributing to the soaplike story line, that fact would determine whether Buffy could be rescued Lois Lane–style, in mid-fall, from a church steeple, or whether she'd be smeared all over the nearest gravestone. It would figure prominently in any episode featuring a tête-à-tête at Buffy's bedroom window. It was an artistic choice

## Who Was That?

EPISODE PRODUCTION NUMBERS: PART 1, "WELCOME TO THE HELLMOUTH," 4V01

PART 2, "THE HARVEST," 4V02

ORIGINAL AIR DATE: MARCH 10, 1997

WRITTEN BY: JOSS WHEDON

DIRECTED BY: PART 1, CHARLES MARTIN SMITH

PART 2, JOHN T. KRETCHMER

### CAST

| | |
|---|---|
| Buffy Summers | Sarah Michelle Gellar |
| Xander (Alexander) Harris | Nicholas Brendon |
| Willow Rosenberg | Alyson Hannigan |
| Cordelia (Cordy) Chase | Charisma Carpenter |
| Rupert Giles | Anthony Stewart Head |

### GUEST CAST

| | |
|---|---|
| The Master | Mark Metcalf |
| Luke | Brian Thompson |
| Angel (Angelus) | David Boreanaz |
| Principal Bob Flutie | Ken Lerner |
| Mrs. Joyce Summers | Kristine Sutherland |
| Darla | Julie Benz |
| Thomas "Debarge" | J. Patrick Lawlor |
| Jesse | Eric Balfour |
| Teacher | Natalie Strauss |
| Girl #1 | Amy Chance |
| Girl #2 | Tupelo Jereme |
| Girl #3 | Persia White |
| Girl #4 | Deborah Brown |
| Harmony | Mercedes McNab |
| Guy in the Computer Class | Jeffrey Steven Smith |
| Bouncer | Teddy Lane Jr. |
| Boy | Carmine D. Giovinazzo |

5. Which series premiere actor later returned in a completely different role?

A. Brian Thompson
B. Mark Metcalf
C. Seth Green
D. David Boreanaz

**ANSWERS**

1. B

2. A

3. D

4. D

5. A

that, all by itself, simultaneously made a whole series of future scenes unworkable while enabling an entirely different line of dramatic action. Any writer caught trying to trap Angel in the bottom of open wells, mine shafts, or hidden subway entrances would quickly earn the scorn of attentive fans.

Fortunately, the Buffyverse seems firmly set in the Western vampire tradition, established by Bram Stoker, and, so far, hasn't veered into some of the more exotic versions of vampires such as the disembodied Malay model, which is noteworthy more for its single nostril than its bloodsucking. Interesting audiences in a vamp that preferred rice wine to the raw ingredients for blood pudding would be a tough sell, as would trying to keep track of the can's and can't's for the 114 distinct vampire types recognized by the Society of Historical Vampiric Study alone. Linking major events, such as Drusilla's successful reunion with her sire and the Master's original imprisonment, to churches strongly suggests that future episodes will adhere to the Christian-Demonic worldview, which potential fans relate to most easily.

Christian-Demonic? Yup. The early Christian church had more demons than angels. Demons caused disease, madness, and even children's nose-picking. "The devil made me do it" remains our modern cliché for a belief taken much more seriously between the fourth and sixteenth centuries A.D. "On the Rising of the Dead and the Cursing of Demons," a monastic paper written in the tenth century by a chap known only as Benedito the Thin, puts forward the common belief rather succinctly:

> The rising of the dead, especially on full or new moon, indicates the possession by demons of the deceased prior to death but, obviously, after the administration of the Last Sacraments. Therefore, it behooves the local lay minister to withhold Final Rites until it is clear that the penitent is indeed about to die, affording as little opportunity as possible for the demon to take over the dying. Performing the Sacrament in daylight, and observing the penitent's death before the next sunset is, of course, proof against any possibility of possession, thus assuring the undisturbed rest of the deceased.

Fortunately for television-series viewers and creators, the Western vampire tradition is flush with its own history and inter-

## Everything I Ever Needed to Know, I Learned from *Buffy*

† Avoid necking with dates who take
shortcuts through cemeteries.

† "Pepper spray is so passé."—Buffy

† The dead rising really should rate an assembly.

† Never call your principal by his first name—
even if he asks you to.

† A dead guy in a locker works better than
a fire alarm for canceling gym class.

nal disagreements, all of which give us room to play. While holy water is as potent a weapon for Buffy as it was for Van Helsing, she has yet to deal with a shape-shifting vampire, or some vampires' nasty habit of turning gaseous just as they are about to be staked. Though Giles decided to toss out *The Slayer's Handbook* after meeting Buffy, Kendra—that other one-and-only Vampire Slayer— probably read the ink right off hers, and Kendra had no doubt whatsoever that Angel wouldn't be able to drift through the bars of the trap she arranged for him or turn himself into a more convenient-size bat or rodent to fly or scamper out.

Crucifixes don't figure in the Western vampire myths until 1897, when Stoker added them to the Slayer arsenal. Since then, the simpler symbol of the cross has served as proof positive against vampires in sources as diverse as *Nosferatu*, a silent film from Germany, and *The Case of the Sussex Vampire*, a chilling Sherlock Holmes tale, which came out two years after *Nosferatu*, in 1924. Over the next seventy years, anything even vaguely resembling a cross seemed to work in warding off the undead, including a pair of crossed plastic forks in that underground vampire-movie classic, *To Have and Have Not: A Vampire in McDonald's*, produced for exactly $112 in 1977 as a parody of Anne Rice's wildly popular *Interview with the Vampire*. The Master, while trapped in his underground parish, almost came to terms with the huge cross buried with him, but few other Sunnydale vamps evidenced any resistance to the symbol whatsoever. That weakness is probably what prompted Angel to present Buffy with her own cross, a weakness he proves equally susceptible to when his passionate clinch with Buffy results in a cross-shaped burn on his chest. In fact, most things religious, or at least Christian, consistently freak out Sunnydale vamps. Even the consecrated ground of the cemetery proved painful to the manicures of the vampires digging up the Master's bones.

As Buffy and Angel have yet to enjoy a normal date, we've no idea if he'll prove as susceptible to the garlic in her Caesar salad, but his offscreen encounter with a "Gypsy curse," which gave him back his soul, once again harkens back to Stoker's book, the basis for the Western vampire. Whether the Gypsies who acted as the Count's servants were actually protected from his more lusty vagaries or not is never clearly stated, but they'd certainly have insight into this strange being's habits, enough to make them logical players in the life of Angelus, a vampire reputed to be well over the age of majority.

Unlike garlic, silver crosses, and Eucharistic elements such as

The quintessential vampire, Bela Lugosi, in *Dracula*, 1931. Angel's come a long way, baby!

holy water and wafers, mirrors hold a contradictory reputation in vampiric folklore. In Rudyard Kipling's "The Vampire," which appeared the same year as Bram Stoker's *Dracula* did, vampires were fascinated by their reflections. Numerous east-Indian and other Asian tales featured vampires undone by their narcissistic interest in their own images. A *ginn*, an aquatic version of a genie, hauls one vampire into a river after the bloodsucker stops to peer at his own reflection in the water. In a Korean take on the tale, the vampire is held fast, mesmerized by his own appearance in the silver mirror of a soon-to-be victim. The reflection of the rising sun bouncing off the mirror and into his face makes any further attacks highly unlikely, and the victim will later defend herself against a charge of vanity by explaining how the mirror had been used to save the remaining members of the household from the vampire.

Kipling, influenced by his own Eastern experiences, probably found Stoker's vampires rather odd creatures. Instead of being entranced by their own appearances, Stoker's vampires cast no reflection at all and abhorred mirrors. A nifty, not to mention cheap, effect, Angel's lack of reflection has been featured nearly a dozen times in opening episodes of the *Buffy* series. Oddly enough, if the Buffyverse followed Stoker's reasoning as well as his example, Angel might well be noteworthy for actually *having* a reflection after all. Stoker's fantastic tale suggested that mirrors had a metaphysical ability to reflect the state of a person's soul, his conscience. Of all the vampires encountered in the series so far, only Angel shows any remorse. While he may not possess his own soul, he definitely has a conscience.

*Buffy the Vampire Slayer,* usually noted for its portrayal of internally consistent vampires, did, for a while, seem unable to adopt one model or the other. In its portrayal of Angel, and later Spike, *Buffy* created the quintessential darkling seducer. Like a host of charismatic vamps before him, Angel exudes an unworldly attraction for the woman in his unlife. Deep, dark eyes and the not-so-subtle hint of danger have attracted fictional women to vampires since the first silent films. Adding a low husky voice that would be spiced chocolate if voices had flavors simply enhanced the mystique well into the talkie era. Though much vampire fiction is heavily indebted to Bram Stoker's original book, Stoker's antihero had

## Written on the Wall

One of the actors in the premiere episodes of *Buffy the Vampire Slayer* is an experienced film vampire. Brian Thompson had just finished a stint on *Kindred: The Embraced,* in which he played Eddie Fiori, before being cast as Luke, the Master's chosen Vessel.

\* \* \*

Sunnydale High School looking just too familiar? It's Torrance High, the same school featured in *Beverly Hills 90210.* Gives you a whole new view of the zip code, doesn't it?

\* \* \*

Love continuity bloopers? Watch the books that Rupert tries to foist on Buffy. In one shot, the titles face Buffy; in the next, they face Giles, then back again! Not enough? Watch the bouncer at The Bronze. Though Cordelia states quite clearly that there's "no cover charge," the bouncer's taking money from those in the lineup outside! While The Bronze may be the only nightclub in town, how likely is it that the patrons were bribing their way into a cockroach-infested dance bar in the "bad part of town"?

\* \* \*

nothing in common with the pale but gorgeous crew inhabiting underground caverns in Rice's *Interview with the Vampire,* the sexy Old-Country gentleman in *The Brides of Dracula,* or even the well-coiffed Spike. Stoker's Dracula reeked of age, decay, and depravity. In creating the Master, the antithesis of the distinctly sexual characters of Angel, Spike, and Drusilla, the Buffyverse embraces both versions found in Western vampire lore.

# "The Witch"

the short version

Every Vampire Slayer needs a hobby, right? Buffy, nostalgic for normalcy, seeking a trace of her pre-Slayer life, decides to try out for the cheerleading squad. There's no sign of vampires there, but when a talented cheerer suddenly bursts into flames at the first tryout, it's clear that something evil is at work. As squad member after squad member succumbs to increasingly bizarre attacks, Buffy and her fellow hopeful, Amy, move ever closer to the hallowed position of pom-pom shaker. When Buffy, not Amy, makes the team, the Slayer quickly becomes the next target.

## The Finer Points of Witch Detection

the longer look

From the beginning it was obvious that a small-screen Buffy would have to be a little more versatile than her big-screen predecessor so it's proven rather convenient that Sunnydale, sitting on its mystical-convergence point, also attracts any number of other nasties to keep audiences amused and Buffy guessing. Just when she figures she's got the find 'em–stake 'em routine down pat, just when she's beginning to get a bit blasé about the whole thing, along comes a witch to stretch her slaying skills.

Luckily for Buffy, and cheerleaders everywhere, Xander, Willow, and Giles didn't need a particularly big library to find

11

## QUESTIONS

1. Which *Buffy the Vampire Slayer* regular was named for an Avon perfume?

   A. Charisma Carpenter
   B. Joss Whedon
   C. Seth Green
   D. Kristine Sutherland

2. For which movie screenplay *wasn't* Joss Whedon an uncredited writer?

   A. *Twister*
   B. *Toy Story*
   C. *Waterworld*
   D. *Speed*

3. Which of the following TV shows *didn't* feature vampires?

   A. *Kolchak: The Night Stalker*
   B. *NightMan*
   C. *Dark Shadows*
   D. *Forever Knight*

4. Which *Buffy the Vampire Slayer* character was named after a "really mean girl" Joss Whedon's wife once knew?

   A. Amy
   B. Marcie
   C. Harmony
   D. Cordelia

a host of ways to identify and destroy witches. Witch-hunters have been refining and documenting their stalking techniques with a fervor to challenge even that of a Watcher.

For those without the resources of a biology-chemistry lab like Sunnydale's, which just happens to stock mercury, nitric acid, and eye of newt, there was a low-tech solution called "ducking." No quacking, but plenty of screaming probably accompanied this bizarre ritual that required the suspected witch be tied to a stool pretzel-style, right thumb to left big toe, and dumped into the nearest decent-size body of water. In Christianity, water symbolizes the baptismal sacraments, and it was believed that water would reject the devil-worshipping witch, the only type of pagan in medieval times, and send her bobbing back to the surface. No one seemed to notice that anyone tied in that particular position—the same position rescue personnel suggest to conserve body heat and energy if you happen to find yourself without a boat in the middle of the ocean—would float anyway! If the witch managed to defy the laws of physics and actually sank, she usually drowned before onlookers could tug her out, but as drowning was unassailable proof of the person's innocence, she could at least be buried within the confines of a consecrated cemetery. Small comfort there.

Variations of the ducking stool abounded, mostly dictated by local geography and imagination. The community unlucky enough to have a shallow stream instead of a nice deep river or pond needed some other model of a ducking stool, usually a contraption much like a seesaw. The victim would be strapped to the end of the board, usually head down, and swiftly plunged into whatever water was available, while her inquisitors began reciting biblical passages or prayers over her submerged figure. It was a double whammy for the "witch." Early forensic investigators who uncovered the methods of England's Brides-in-the-Bathtub killer discovered that dunking a person headfirst into water, especially by pulling their heels over their heads, can kill her almost instantly! Even if the accused survived the initial plunge, the witch-hunter invariably chose the longest commonly used prayer known within the community and asked the slowest speaker to intone it. Naturally, few witches escaped the ducking stool. Luckily for Amy, Sunnydale High is a

**Bubble, bubble, toil and trouble. Every witch needs a good cauldron.**

5. **In what year was the novel *Dracula* published?**

    A. 1816
    B. 1888
    C. 1897
    D. 1901

statistical anomaly. Until the swim team turned into sea monsters, no one knew SHS had a pool!

Witch-prickers were common weapons in the witch-hunter's arsenal as well. In fact, the truly enthusiastic hunter usually sported a matched pair of the nasty blades. It was widely believed that the witch, in consorting with the devil to achieve her unholy powers, was endowed by him with a Witch's Mark. The Mark could be almost anything, a birthmark, a small scar, or a mole. In several cases the witch-hunter claimed the Mark was an extra nipple from which a familiar might feed. (Owning a pet of any type was, of course, a perfectly legitimate reason to suspect someone of witchcraft.) Regardless of the form it took, the Mark was, of course, hidden from normal sight and required the witch-hunter to strip the

ANSWERS

1. A

2. B

3. B

4. D

5. C

## Who Was That?

**EPISODE PRODUCTION NUMBER: 4V03**

**ORIGINAL AIR DATE: MARCH 17, 1997**

**WRITTEN BY: DANA RESTON**

**DIRECTED BY: STEPHEN CRAGG**

### CAST

| | |
|---|---|
| Buffy Summers | Sarah Michelle Gellar |
| Xander Harris | Nicholas Brendon |
| Willow Rosenberg | Alyson Hannigan |
| Cordelia Chase | Charisma Carpenter |
| Rupert Giles | Anthony Stewart Head |

### GUEST CAST

| | |
|---|---|
| Mrs. Joyce Summers | Kristine Sutherland |
| Amy | Elizabeth Anne Allen |
| Catherine the Great | Robin Riker |
| Mr. Pole | Jim Doughan |
| Lishanne | Nicole Prescott |
| Senior Cheerleader | Amanda Wilmshurst |
| Dr. Gregory | William Monaghan |

penitent naked and shave off all her body hair before examining her entire body, especially her most private parts. Given by the devil himself, the Mark reputedly was resistant to physical harm. It could be stabbed repeatedly without causing the victim any pain or even drawing blood. The number of witches so discovered seems incredibly high until one remembers that witch-hunters routinely carried *two* prickers. Inevitably, the one used on himself or another witness drew blood; the other, however, fitted with a retracting blade to rival anything Hollywood would dream up later, could be plunged into the offending mark for eternity and never leave a mark or drop of blood. Not really an option for the Slayerettes though. After all, even Sunnydale's dull-witted students would probably notice that Buffy was stabbing a classmate in the middle of the chemistry lab.

Staking the supposed witch out was yet another method for the poorly equipped inquisitors. The naked witch, strapped to the bare ground in a suitable cell or even out in the town square, was encouraged to endlessly repeat some Christian prayer, the Our Father or the Apostles' Creed being particularly popular choices, throughout an entire night. If, at any time between sunset and sunrise, she stopped speaking, buckets of cold water were thrown on her until she began again. The true test wasn't in oration, however. No, if despite the witch's invocation of God's name, she were approached by any living creature, be it a cockroach or a cat or, more commonly in most colonial settings, a rat, the visitation was a sure sign that the devil, through his imp in familiar form, was attempting to wrest the witch's soul back to him. (The Bronze's clientele, before the fumigation party, wouldn't have had a chance.) The fact that most villages were infested with vermin of one sort or another did nothing to mitigate her guilt.

The profusion of Christian symbols used to root out witches raised absolutely no eyebrows in the medieval and colonial periods. Witches were assumed to be agents of the Christian devil, possibly

---

## Everything I Ever Needed to Know, I Learned from *Buffy*

† "I laugh in the face of danger—then I hide
until it goes away!"—Xander

† Nothing good ever happened in a high-school locker room.

† Barbie—the natural tool of evil magicians.

† Scantily clad girls in revealing postures are the central
figures in the religion of pubescent high-school boys.

15

**A little eye of newt and wing of bat, just what every high-school bio-chem lab should carry!**

his mistresses, certainly his coconspirators in any evil perpetrated against their neighbors. The most blatant test of this consensus was "the Scales," particularly popular in the United States. Some communities maintained huge scales just for this purpose, but where such devices didn't exist, any plank that could be balanced over something else made an adequate substitute. With the community gathered to watch, the unfortunate suspect was perched on one side of the scales or one end of the plank. A Bible was then laid on the opposing side, and if the Scales balanced, the woman was cleared of any wrongdoing as she was obviously being buoyed up by God's favor. There are no recorded cases of anyone passing the test, though a large cat was convicted by just this practice in Rhode

## Written on the Wall

If you think the portrayal of killer cheerleaders was over the top, think again! In Texas, a mother became so obsessed with her daughter obtaining a spot on the high school's spirit squad that she hired her brother-in-law to kill her daughter's competition, coincidentally also named Amber, and the girl's mother! The price of this piece of upward mobility? Two big-carat diamond earrings.

\* \* \*

Amber's stunt double forgot to put on the long wig before Buffy played firefighter on her hands!

\* \* \*

Sunnydale High School must be feeling the budget crunch. Why else would they use Driver's Education cars without brakes on the teacher's side?

\* \* \*

Catch the *1996 Cheer Leading Tryouts* sign in the gym scenes? It might look weird, but it makes perfect sense if you realize that the episode would have aired in the fall of '96 if *Buffy the Vampire Slayer* had premiered in September instead of as a '97 mid-season replacement.

\* \* \*

What do you think the chances are that Catherine the Great was a Madison before *and after* her marriage? That's the only way "Catherine Madison" could captain the spirit squad *and* have a daughter named Amy Madison.

\* \* \*

Island in 1786. Some inventive communities even managed to streamline the conviction-punishment process. Their Scales are reputed to have been made of metal and a charcoal fire was laid beneath the witch's half of the setup just prior to the test. As she sank, she was literally fried alive. Alongside these barbaric rituals, splashing a little eye-of-newt concoction on a classmate to see if it turns blue seems downright civilized.

A very few traditional tests for witchery were considerably more subtle, however, and might have been a tad less obvious than stealing Amy's hair from her brush to see if it turned blue when exposed to newts. Four-leaf clovers were known to wilt in the presence of witches, as were bleeding-heart plants, roses, and lavender. Like Eastern vampires, witches were believed to be highly sexual creatures, susceptible to anything that played on their vanity. Therefore, it was obvious that women carrying mirrors secreted on their person—in their purse or pocket, for example—were likely to be witches. Women found staring at their reflection in a pool of water could expect to be ducked in even more water later. And any woman showing a hint of interest in any man, even her husband, was held to be displaying the moral lassitude likely to be found in the devil's handmaids. Think there might have been a mirror lurking in Amy's bag, too?

Of course, if the television Buffy had the same PMS problem as the film Slayer had whenever she came close to a demon, the TV Buffy might well have been a superbitch around Amy. After all, every medieval witch-hunter knew that witches were just as demon-possessed as their vampire kin!

EPISODE:

# "Teacher's Pet"

the short version

uffy and Willow would have to be blind not to notice that Xander, and every other boy at school, is falling for the substitute biology teacher, Ms. Natalie French. Of course, they'd also have to be blind and *nasally impaired* not to notice the previous biology teacher, or at least most of him, hanging in the school's walk-in fridge. Xander, however, refuses to see any connection between the two instructors, even when his equally hormone-driven friends start disappearing after their extracurricular sessions with the sexy sub.

## Virgins: The Endangered Species

the longer look

It almost goes without saying that you just can't write a show like *Buffy the Vampire Slayer* and *not* touch on sex or virginity once in a while. Even putting aside the major roles such topics play in a teen's social life, you'd be hard pressed to find some aspect of the weirdness attracted to Sunnydale that doesn't center around who's having sex and who's not. Frankly, despite all the "Wait" advertising out there, residents of Buffy's little square acre probably didn't have much incentive to hang on to their physical innocence—even before Ms. French came to town.

**Wouldn't you look twice if your best friend was dating a praying mantis?**

Traditionally, virgins make the best sacrifices. Got a volcano about to blow up? No problem. Toss in a luscious virgin decked in local greenery and call it a day. Need some glimpses into the future before a big battle? Too easy. Slice open the nearest unbred goat and see which way its entrails fall onto the ground. Really big battle? Try the same thing on one of your virgin daughters. Monsoon god to placate? Nothing like a virgin wrapped in linen (presumably to prevent swimming) and tossed into the nearest river to slow the rising waters. Makes sex with a giant, shape-shifting bug seem almost trivial, doesn't it? Perhaps the fact that so few virgin victims were *male* lulled Xander into that "false sense of security" thing. Silly boy.

20

The infamous Erszebet Bathory, countess of one of Transylvania's wealthiest sixteenth-century families, thought the blood of nubile young virgins could keep her forever young, but since she wasn't a vampire in the strictest sense of the word, she reputedly found new ways to try her virgin-blood theory out. Though the facts are now muddled, Erszebet Bathory killed between a dozen and four hundred young women—and a few handsome young men of Xander's age—over the course of her life, mostly by slitting their throats as they leaned over her bathtub. Not only was this a tidier alternative to chewing their heads off or biting their necks, it allowed her to indulge her real pleasure, bathing her entire body in their warm blood. Remembered best for her bloodbaths, Bathory was actually convicted of a host of other crimes against the pretty virgins who flowed through her household, not the least of which was throwing them naked into the snows of the Carpathian Mountains and pouring buckets of cold water over them before driving them off into the woods with her dogs at their heels.

Virginity, or a lack thereof, profoundly affected the career options open to Golden-Era Greek girls entering the temples and oracular sites. Anyone was eligible to light lanterns and scrub floors; only virgins could be indoctrinated into the realms of prophecy and priestesshood. The Oracle at Delphi didn't need any particular gift to discern what would happen to her if she lost her virginal status. She'd be tossed down into the same pit from which those vision-inducing intoxicating fumes rose. Vestal virgins at the temple of Apollo either stayed virgins or looked forward to the Ritual of a Hundred Blades. You'd almost think one or two would be enough, wouldn't you? Nope, reports of the very few occasions when the punishment was enacted strongly indicate the fallen woman was kept alive for the full hundred strokes.

Celibacy, if not virginity, is still a requirement for many religious orders. Roman Catholic priests and nuns are the most obvious examples, but dozens of other modern groups make similar, if temporary, demands of their members. The Church of Inner Transformation is a Californian sect whose handsome young male "priests" are required to refrain from sexual practices for two days before cel-

### QUESTIONS

1. Who has never portrayed a faculty member on *Buffy the Vampire Slayer*?

   A. Brian Thompson
   B. Armin Shimerman
   C. Ken Lerner
   D. Robia La Morte

2. Which *Buffy the Vampire Slayer* regular was once sued by McDonald's?

   A. Charisma Carpenter
   B. Sarah Michelle Gellar
   C. Anthony Stewart Head
   D. Nicholas Brendon

3. Who is the only regular cast member of *Buffy the Vampire Slayer* with a twin brother?

   A. Anthony Stewart Head
   B. Nicholas Brendon
   C. David Boreanaz
   D. Seth Green

4. Which performer's music hasn't been featured on *Buffy the Vampire Slayer*?

   A. Velvet Chain
   B. The Flamingoes
   C. Splendid
   D. Marilyn Manson

## Who Was That?

EPISODE PRODUCTION NUMBER: 4V04
ORIGINAL AIR DATE: MARCH 24, 1997
WRITTEN BY: DAVID GREENWALT
DIRECTED BY: BRUCE SETH GREEN

### CAST

| | |
|---|---|
| Buffy Summers | Sarah Michelle Gellar |
| Xander Harris | Nicholas Brendon |
| Willow Rosenberg | Alyson Hannigan |
| Cordelia Chase | Charisma Carpenter |
| Rupert Giles | Anthony Stewart Head |
| Angel | David Boreanaz |

### GUEST CAST

| | |
|---|---|
| Principal Bob Flutie | Ken Lerner |
| Ms. French, a.k.a. She-Mantis | Musetta Vander |
| Blayne | Jackson Price |
| Older, Real Natalie French | Jean Speegle Howard |
| Dr. Gregory | William Monaghan |
| Homeless Guy | Jack Knight |
| Teacher | Michael Robb Verona |
| Bud #1 | Karim Oliver |

ebrating masses. Muslim men periodically abstain from sex, even after marriage, while furthering their religious studies. Even for a violation of temporary vows, the punishments remain harsh.

Xander shouldn't feel totally demoralized by his virginal state. Despite the misery virgins endured over the ages, virginity also somehow became associated with luck. Knights who went into their first battles as virgins (rather unlikely, but what the hell?) were destined to come home *with* their shields rather than *on* them. Kind of makes you wonder if that's why athletes are told to abstain before a big game, doesn't it? The blood of virgins held mystical powers if it was handled by a priest, and it has been implicated in miracles of all types. Magicians scrying in a bowl of virgin's tears saw true visions. Unicorns, apparently as adept at sniffing out virgins as Ms. French, could only be captured by virgins with valiant quests. A lock of a virgin's hair also provided protection from more common ills such as venereal disease. How it was lucky for the virgins who were being bled, shorn, and induced to cry bowlfuls of tears is, of course, questionable.

The quest for a virgin has been the subject of numerous horror films. Stories involving young girls drained of their blood and sac-

5. **Which of the following isn't an ethnic equivalent of "vampire"?**

   A. Bruxsa
   B. Kolchak
   C. Lamia
   D. Vampyr

## Everything I Ever Needed to Know, I Learned from *Buffy*

† "Powerful laxatives" are an integral part of delayed psychotherapy.

† Admitting your middle name is Lavelle does nothing for your dating status.

† "Needs should definitely be met—as long as it doesn't require ointments the next day."—Xander

† Your dates shouldn't have serrated fingers.

† Even old men who believe their mothers are Pekingese and who howl at the moon regularly can still be right.

† Recording bat sonar is best done by deaf librarians.

† There's nothing scarier than the contents of a school cafeteria fridge—even without beheaded biology teachers taking up shelf space.

† Picket palings make good stakes in a pinch.

**ANSWERS**

1. A

2. B

3. B

4. D

5. B

## Written on the Wall

It's no wonder Dr. Gregory couldn't recognize the She-Mantis! He couldn't even tell an ant from a tiger beetle in his own slide collection!

★　★　★

The continuity errors . . . well, they continue. Keep a sharp eye on Ms. French's sleeves as she prepares her odd lunch. Up. Down. Up. You'd think she had her hands too occupied with that sandwich to be adjusting her cuffs, wouldn't you?

★　★　★

rificed for obscure magical rituals are practically passé after almost a hundred years of films made by all sorts of directors. Spoofs such as *Once Bitten,* the tale of a vampire family's search for that rarest of creatures, a male virgin, made hysterical use of the stereotype, as did the usually staid *X-Files* in an episode called "Syzygy," in which two teens used the virgin scenario as a reason to hit on the class stud.

How sex—and the lack of sex—became a common thread among witchcraft, Christianity, vampire folklore, ancient prophets, and giant, mate-eating She-Mantises is likely grounded in those Earth religions that have mostly faded from our collective Western consciousness. Practitioners of Hindu tantric yoga, Buddhism in the Tibetan tradition, the Ordo Templi Orientis rites, and the infamous rituals of Aleister Crowley all include sexual magic in their ceremonial options. Most theories identify sexual magic with an attempt to unite with the Goddess, to bond with the universe, to share the energy of an encompassing life force. Western theology identified sexual activity with original sin, so, while dozens of "pagan" rituals, dates, and beliefs were integrated into Christianity, sexual magic remained taboo.

In Victorian times, this severe repression of sexual topics resulted in two clearly related events: the rise of dozens of "theosophical societies," which might well be described as occult clubs for Victorian gentry, and the startling popularity of all manner of plays, books, and even poetry on vampires, werewolves, incubi, and succubi, all of whom were portrayed as charismatic and highly sexual beings, capable of attracting virginal victims of both sexes.

Like Buffy doesn't have enough relationship problems?

# EPISODE:

# "Never Kill a Boy on the First Date"

Saving the universe from periodic outbreaks of insidious evil is all very good—for the universe!—but it doesn't do much for the average Slayer's social life. Buffy discovers just how inconvenient preordination can be when Giles's latest research indicates that her very first Sunnydale date coincides with an ancient prophecy's claim that the Slayer will be led into Hell the same night! Juggling her secret identity and her social calendar gets downright hairy when her latest romantic interest doesn't run screaming when the vamps show up.

the short version

## In the Club: The Case for Secret Identities

**Giles:** *If your identity as a Slayer is revealed, it could put you and all those around you in grave danger.*
**Buffy:** *Well, in that case, I won't wear my button that says, "I'm a Slayer, ask me how!"*

the longer look

If comic books and television shows are the ultimate authorities on superheroes and, more recently, superheroines, then a secret identity is an absolute prerequisite for saving the world from any number of nasties.

Episodes such as "Angel," which features Mrs. Summers as

27

## Who Was That?

**EPISODE PRODUCTION NUMBER: 4V05**

**ORIGINAL AIR DATE: MARCH 31, 1997**

**WRITTEN BY: ROBERT DES HOTEL AND DEAN BATALI**

**DIRECTED BY: DAVID SEMEL**

### CAST

| | |
|---|---|
| Buffy Summers | Sarah Michelle Gellar |
| Xander Harris | Nicholas Brendon |
| Willow Rosenberg | Alyson Hannigan |
| Cordelia Chase | Charisma Carpenter |
| Rupert Giles | Anthony Stewart Head |
| The Master | Mark Metcalf |
| Angel | David Boreanaz |

### GUEST CAST

| | |
|---|---|
| Owen Thurman | Christopher Wiehl |
| Militia Guy | Geoff Meed |
| Van Driver | Robert Mont |
| Boy | Andrew J. Ferchland |

an appetizer for Darla (the Master's favorite female vamp), and "When She Was Bad," in which Buffy's best friend, her Watcher, and her computer-science teacher dangle like sides of beef inside a vampire lair awaiting execution, begin to make a case for keeping Buffy's extracurricular activities quiet. Episodes such as "Never Kill a Boy on the First Date" drive the point home faster than even Buffy can swing a stake.

While Giles is something of a chronic worrywart, a tad obsessive, and maybe even anal-retentive, he seems to have some basis for upping the insurance premiums on those about to join the ranks of the "Slayerettes." Owen, Buffy's one living date, just shouldn't have "asked her how." Buffy's friends tend to end up in some interesting, not to mention deadly, little spots from week to week.

For instance, Xander may avoid the joys of being hung upside down prior to exsanguination in "When She Was Bad," but he's been up to his neck in other forms of danger since he first uttered the immortal phrase, "Can I have you?" to the New Girl. Take his first crush on an older woman in "Teacher's Pet." Ms. French might have had the creepy-crawlies section of the biology curriculum down pat, but she might also have had Xander for supper! Girls his own age don't work out any better in "Inca Mummy Girl." Then there's that whole growling-sniffing phase in "The Pack." Like that happens to everyone you know? True, Buffy didn't actually cause any bug-women to pick Sunnydale as their nesting site, or personally arrange for a Peruvian exhibit to come to the local museum. Still, once they arrived, she decided to step right in and rid the

---

## Everything I Ever Needed to Know, I Learned from *Buffy*

† Calculations, even the most precise, are bad, bad, bad when they interfere with a first date.

† "Flat tire" is a better beg-off for a broken date than "I was sitting in a cemetery with the librarian waiting for a vampire to rise so I could prevent an evil prophecy from coming to pass."

† "A cranky Slayer is a careless Slayer."—Buffy

† Dating a guy who likes slaying more than Emily Dickinson probably won't work, even if he is dating a Slayer.

† Post-mortem twitching aside, dead bodies are supposed to stay under their sheets.

† Never schedule a date to coincide with major vampiric prophecies.

### QUESTIONS

1. **Of the following, which one isn't an honest-to-goodness produced film of vampire romance?**

   A. *Muffy the Vampire Layer*

   B. *Wanda Does Transylvania*

   C. *Bite!*

   D. *Moon Light Enchantment*

2. **Who portrayed the Watcher in the original Buffy film?**

   A. Anthony Stewart Head

   B. Donald Sutherland

   C. Joss Whedon

   D. Charlton Heston

3. **Which *Buffy the Vampire Slayer* regular had a starring role in *My Stepmother Is an Alien*?**

   A. Seth Green

   B. Alyson Hannigan

   C. Charisma Carpenter

   D. Robia La Morte

4. **Which real place has *not* been a shooting location for *Buffy the Vampire Slayer*?**

   A. San Diego Zoo

   B. Disneyland

   C. Torrence High School

   D. The Rose Garden

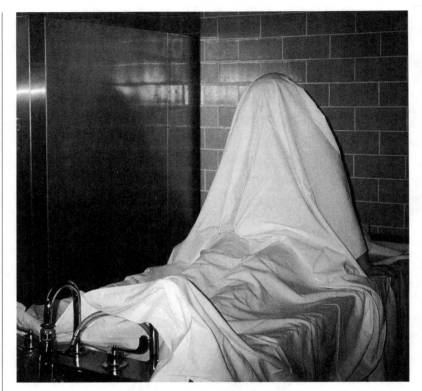

No, corpses *aren't* supposed to move!

neighborhood of yet more forms of mystic convergence–dependent life forms.

Willow, the original Slayerette, has certainly been filling more pages in her diary since Buffy's arrival. Before she became best buddies with a Slayer, heartfelt accounts of her latest nonevent with Xander took up most of the writing space. But after Willow meets Buffy, there's a demon who thinks Willow would make a great date; the vampires who take out her best friends in the Audiovisual Club, and the aforementioned attempt to sacrifice her and raise the Master once again.

Of course, it's not just Buffy's nearest and dearest who've had reason to question their relationship with the New Girl. There's Cordelia. In less than a full school year, she's blinded by a vindictive witch with a yen for pom-poms; nearly fed to a really ugly "Reptile Boy" at an otherwise mostly normal frat party; attacked by an invisible girl who wanted to create a lasting impression on the May Queen's face; and comes close to getting beheaded by a pair of young Frankensteins and her old—almost cold—beau. And that doesn't include her numerous encounters with vampires! Not bad for someone who has yet to even be seen in actual public contact with Buffy.

Makes you wonder when the general student body is going to make the connection between the New Girl and the sudden rash of deaths among their classmates. With the present rate of attrition among Sunnydale co-eds, Buffy won't have to worry about getting a date for the senior prom—there won't be enough students left to take out to Taco Bell! In the first thirty-two episodes alone, dozens of Sunnydale's teens meet rather gory ends. The series opened with a dead guy in a locker and rolls right along, averaging one student

**5. Whose first film was *Over the Brooklyn Bridge*?**

**A. Nicholas Brendon**
**B. Anthony Stewart Head**
**C. Alyson Hannigan**
**D. Sarah Michelle Gellar**

**Where Giles spent the evening while Buffy had the First Owen Date.**

31

**ANSWERS**

1. D

2. B

3. B

4. B

5. D

## Written on the Wall

Where did the beeper Buffy confounds Giles with come from? She sure didn't pull it out of her pocket—or his! Watching the scene twice reveals that she must have picked it out of the air. There's absolutely nowhere else it could have come from!

\* \* \*

death per episode. Even assuming Sunnydale has a fairly healthy enrollment, statistics like that start to add up. "PCP" and "gang violence" just won't cover as explanations forever.

And, even if the students haven't begun putting stakes and bodies together just yet, the staff—several of whom witness Buffy's slaying skills in action during "School Hard"—should. Like, what investigative analysis wouldn't find something significant in having one biology teacher decapitated by the French instructor; another teacher smothered by an invisible girl; your technopagan computer-science teacher taken over by demons; and your principal eaten by hyena-possessed students a little off the curve? The substitute teachers of Sunnydale might be grinning, but why isn't the rest of the staff looking for jobs in friendlier environs? Like Siberia, maybe.

Maybe Giles is right: Sunnydalians don't actually want to know what's going on. They're willing to re-create their memories to exclude those things that don't fit. Things like "gang members" with bizarre facial features. Things like cemeteries that appear and disappear. Things like Halloween costumes that mask personalities as well as faces. Things like floating baseball bats and flaming pompoms.

Or maybe they're just stupid.

After all, Clark fooled Lois with nothing more than a pair of glasses and a shy smile.

EPISODE:
# "The Pack"

As Sunnydale continues to attract all things weird, Buffy and pals go on that pregraduation version of a road trip—the school field trip. Everything seems to be going as planned: The teacher has been successfully ditched; the students have reverted to their normal cliquish groupings; and the cool kids are picking on the nerds. Same stuff, different location. That is, until the clique even Cordelia isn't tough enough to hang with decides to take torment to a new level. Utter weirdness breaks out when the "in" crew start acting like a pack of dogs, and Xander suddenly becomes their bosom buddy.

the short version

## It's Amazing What You Can Find in Books These Days

It's no surprise that Rupert Giles, with his love of smelly, musty books, would just happen to have a copy of the *Malleus Maleficarum (The Hammer of Witches)* lying about, but it's certainly not on the general reading list anywhere outside Sunnydale High School's library and hasn't enjoyed any serious study for at least a hundred years.

In its heyday, from 1486 to 1669, when it appeared in no less than *thirty* editions, *Malleus Maleficarum* was one of the most

the longer look

33

**Bow-wow?**

influential books of its time. Prior to its appearance on monastery shelves everywhere, witchcraft wasn't as much a religious practice as it was a collection of folklore and remedies and, as such, not even fully within the authority of the Inquisition. The Inquisitors originally acknowledged three basic types of religious offender: the heretic, the apostate, and participants in foreign pagan practices. Heretics, being those who claimed to be Christians while simultaneously professing beliefs counter to the Church's official viewpoint, were dealt with severely, even if their deviations from the accepted doctrine were made in honest ignorance. Apostates, former practitioners who now denounced the Church or even the existence of God, were, not surprisingly, also favorite targets for a religious inquisition. The pagans, however, and until the *Malleus*

34

*Maleficarum* came along this would include witches, were seldom seen as criminals against the Church and were more often the targets of early-style missionaries than of the torturous Inquisitors. Technically, according to the *Malleus Maleficarum,* Buffy, Slayer of vampires, killer of demons, qualifies as a witch!

How did one book start the witch-hunts? By taking a collection of folkloric traditions, vague rumors, and wild, unfounded speculation about a group broadly defined as witches, cataloging the nonsense, tying it all to Satan worship, and proposing all manner of tortures, promises, and practices that they assure the reader "will successfully identify the witch." If the similarity among "confessions" obtained during this period strikes you as uncommonly uniform, it may have had more to do with the proliferation of the *Malleus Maleficarum* than with any actual experiences of the poor wretches forced to confess.

The key tenet of *The Hammer of Witches* was that witchcraft was Satan worship. Once that point had been established, it was easy to propose any number of ways that the witch gained her powers. Jakob Sprenger and Heinrich Kramer, the Dominican monks responsible for this literary instrument of torture, *chose* demonic possession as the most "logical" explanation for the powers witches obtained from their Dark Master. While Giles might make an informed argument, based on firsthand observation, they had absolutely no evidence to support that claim, of course, but with a little compromise here and there, it was an explanation that could be made to fit all their "facts." That anyone could honestly believe waving a dead hare at your neighbor's cattle could immediately kill twenty-three of them, the basis for an actual case prosecuted in Berne, defies our modern logic anyway, but adding the taint of Satanic possession to the hare-waving quickly brought the wrath of a very powerful Church to bear.

So, why was Giles, faced with a pack of teens turned into hyenas, flipping through a book designed to bring witchcraft under the auspices of the Inquisition? Because, to Sprenger and Kramer at least, witchcraft and demonic possession were one and the same problem. After detailing, almost lovingly, the entire magical system of witches as they imagined it, and continuing at some length on

**QUESTIONS**

1. **Who was born April 12, 1971?**

   **A. Charisma Carpenter**
   **B. Nicholas Brendon**
   **C. Alyson Hannigan**
   **D. Sarah Michelle Gellar**

2. **Which *Buffy the Vampire Slayer* regular took home a daytime Emmy in 1995?**

   **A. Charisma Carpenter**
   **B. Nicholas Brendon**
   **C. Alyson Hannigan**
   **D. Sarah Michelle Gellar**

3. **Which of these actors hasn't played Dracula?**

   **A. Bela Lugosi**
   **B. Gary Oldman**
   **C. Louis Jourdan**
   **D. Boris Karloff**

4. **How long does it take to film a single *Buffy the Vampire Slayer* episode?**

   **A. 5 days**
   **B. 8 days**
   **C. 10 days**
   **D. 14 days**

5. **Who, along with Sarah Michelle Gellar, appeared in the miniseries "A Woman Named Jackie"?**

   **A. Mark Metcalf**
   **B. David Boreanaz**
   **C. Anthony Stewart Head**
   **D. Joss Whedon**

# Who Was That?

EPISODE PRODUCTION NUMBER: 4V06

ORIGINAL AIR DATE: APRIL 7, 1997

WRITTEN BY: MATT KIENE AND JOE REINKMEYER

DIRECTED BY: BRUCE SETH GREEN

## CAST

| | |
|---|---|
| Buffy Summers | Sarah Michelle Gellar |
| Xander Harris | Nicholas Brendon |
| Willow Rosenberg | Alyson Hannigan |
| Rupert Giles | Anthony Stewart Head |

## GUEST CAST

| | |
|---|---|
| Principal Bob Flutie | Ken Lerner |
| Lance | Jeff Maynard |
| The Zookeeper | James Stephens |
| Mr. Anderson | David Brisbin |
| Mrs. Anderson | Barbara K. Whinnery |
| Coach Herrold | Gregory White |
| Joey | Justin Jon Ross |
| Adam | Jeffrey Steven Smith |
| Young Woman | Patrese Borem |
| The Pack | Eion Bailey |
| | Michael McRaine |
| | Brian Gross |
| | Jennifer Sky |

the numerous methods of dealing with such newly defined heretics, there are, scattered amongst the other superstitious nonsense, descriptions of practices for freeing the witch from the possession of the demon. Most of them are decidedly less pleasant than the relatively tame rituals enacted by zookeepers and librarians in Sunnydale. The usual fifteenth-century ritual for exorcism of a demon starting by stripping first the clothes, then some of the skin, from the unlucky "supplicant." It frequently ended with a certain degree of burning for whatever might be left of the victim after the torture. Death, while not the stated goal of these rituals, was, more often than not, the result.

Other books and articles of the same period tended to merely repeat the concepts of the *Malleus Maleficarum* in different ways, usually including even more sensational accounts of witchly practices: One book went so far as to suggest that initiation into the witches' coven required the woman to bed down with a goat, a bull, a horse, and a virgin boy all in the same night. A few treatises expanded the definition of possession itself. One, the *Signs and Practises of Involuntary Possession*, appears to have been offered as a sort of sequel to *The Hammer of Witches* and detailed the means by which a witch might cause an enemy to be possessed and force the original soul out of its body. It would take just seconds for a new

ANSWERS

1. B

2. D

3. D

4. B

5. A

## Everything I Ever Needed to Know, I Learned from *Buffy*

† Short ribs should be well cooked. Trichinosis still infects large percentages of American mascots.

† Eating the principal will probably get you more than detention and a few demerits.

† Every field trip has its little snags.

† A guy's blood pressure is more than a friend needs to know.

† The ultimate sign of true teen love? A tingly head.

## Written on the Wall

**Willow shouldn't put such faith in her computer information. Sure, the first few scenes showed hyenas, but the rest were of a different species altogether—the African Wild Dog, which is more closely related to Australian dingoes than to hyenas. Hyenas, after all, are more closely related to cats than to dogs; they even purr! Their closest taxonomic relatives include the mongooses and the meerkats!**

\* \* \*

soul, demonic or animalistic, to fill the spiritual void inside the body. This "transpossession" reputedly accounted for insanity, any number of violent crimes, and "were-ism," the ability of men and women to become wolves, foxes, hares—or even hyenas! While cases of animalistic possession usually depended on the local presence of the animal spirit to be transposed, it wasn't always so.

A case in point involved the German "witch" Bitta Wiesinger, who once traveled extensively with her husband, an importer of southern Mediterranean goods in the later half of the sixteenth century. On returning home, she wrote to a cousin about her own field trip to a zoo outside Jerusalem. There, for the first time, she'd seen white tigers, aardwolves, and, coincidentally to this episode, hyenas. A well-educated woman for her time, she described each creature in vivid images, including her own observations of their behavior. The hyenas, who were fed while she watched, left a strong impression on Bitta Wiesinger, reflected in the sheer number of words she devoted to her descriptions. Her letters would come back to haunt her years later when, widowed, she moved back to her family home, where her pen-pal cousin had remained. Shortly after her relocation, Bitta argued loudly with a meat seller who, she claimed, brought the family rancid cuts. Shortly after that argument, several women of the household were attacked and savagely beaten. Two were bitten by the apparently insane butcher.

In keeping with the frenzied fears of the time, however, it wasn't the butcher who stood trial for the crimes, but Bitta Wiesinger! The butcher, claiming no memory of the events despite being positively identified by two of his victims, did report he'd come over earlier that day, all queer with insatiable thirsts and hungers. For her part, Bitta's cousin couldn't seem to help declaring how very similar the man's actions were to the descriptions Bitta had written some twenty years before. (Who'd need enemies with family like that, right?) Suddenly, Bitta was placed in the hands of the Church, which was eager to try her for involuntary possession of a meat seller.

When other members of the family pled for her release, suggesting it was impossible for Bitta to have sent a hyena's soul into this man without the availability of a hyena, the *Malleus Maleficarum*-inspired *Signs and Practises of Involuntary Possession*

**All the little silver crosses in the world wouldn't have helped Xander avoid the hazards of a school field trip.**

had already accounted for that little problem. It was claimed that by virtue of Bitta's letters to her family, the essence of a hyena, not its soul because only human beings had souls, had been carried back from the Middle East. The fact that her cousin should have such intense memories of the hyena was proof enough that some part of its presence lived on. Bitta Wiesinger, for complaining about poor service, was tortured for eleven days and then burned at the stake on a hill overlooking her home. The butcher was released following her death, and no charges were ever brought against him.

EPISODE:

# "Angel"

**B**uffy's romantic dreams about dark, mysterious Angel turn to nightmares when she discovers him hunched over her mother's bleeding neck in full, demonic, Ugly Face—after she *invited* him inside. Angel's history as Angelus the Vampire demands that Buffy slay him. It's certainly high on Xander and Rupert's list of things to do. Buffy's decision, already tough enough, is further complicated by the involvement of Darla, Angel's ex-lover. Separating the good vamps from the bad vamps may well be a luxury Buffy can't afford.

the short version

## Whither from Here?

The general response to discovering your sister, father, cousin, or aunt has been through the "whole big sucking thing" is universal.

*Kill it!*

A pretty reasonable response when applied to the recently revived. Though Xander's motive in wanting Angel out of

the longer look

**Great abs—especially for a guy pushing two and a half centuries!**

Buffy's life isn't so very ulterior, his immediate urge to destroy yet another vampire is promptly echoed by Rupert Giles.

Vampires suck blood and make more vampires.

Slayers stake 'em and move on.

At least that's the usual routine.

Still, as if to prove you can't judge a book by its cover, or a film by its posters, some writers have spun the sadistically evil vampire into, of all things, a romantic hero! It seems women, not traditional vampire aficionados, can't get enough of the "damaged man" scenarios. Television viewers may remember *Forever Knight*, and the tortured title character Nick Knight, a vampire even older than Angel, who'd recanted his bloodthirsty ways and, like Angel, kept a supply of blood chilling in his refrigerator instead of darting out for a quick bite whenever he liked.

The kind of mythos associated with Nick and the kind associated with Angel were, naturally, quite different from each other. Nick was never possessed by any demons, so the Gypsies couldn't have done much for him anyway. He came to abhor his bloodlust all on his own and, despite, or because of, a continuous hunger, desperately wanted to regain his humanity.

Given the fact that Buffy is the Slayer and not likely to voluntarily let some demon set up residence in her psyche, it would cer-

## Who Was That?

EPISODE PRODUCTION NUMBER: 4V07

ORIGINAL AIR DATE: APRIL 14, 1997

WRITTEN BY: DAVID GREENWALT

DIRECTED BY: SCOTT BRAZIL

### CAST

| | |
|---|---|
| Buffy Summers | Sarah Michelle Gellar |
| Xander Harris | Nicholas Brendon |
| Willow Rosenberg | Alyson Hannigan |
| Rupert Giles | Anthony Stewart Head |

### GUEST CAST

| | |
|---|---|
| The Master | Mark Metcalf |
| Angel | David Boreanaz |
| Mrs. Joyce Summers | Kristine Sutherland |
| Darla | Julie Benz |
| Collin/The Anointed | Andrew J. Ferchland |
| Meanest Vampire | Charles Wesley |

## SLAYER-IN-TRAINING TRIVIA

### QUESTIONS

1. How long does it take to apply David Boreanaz's Ugly Face?

   A. 15 to 30 minutes
   B. 30 to 60 minutes
   C. 60 to 90 minutes
   D. 3 hours

2. Who parked cars at the Beverly Wilshire Hotel pre–*Buffy the Vampire Slayer*?

   A. Nicholas Brendon
   B. Charisma Carpenter
   C. Alyson Hannigan
   D. David Boreanaz

3. Who was born May 16, 1971, in Buffalo, New York?

   A. Nicholas Brendon
   B. Charisma Carpenter
   C. Alyson Hannigan
   D. David Boreanaz

4. Traditionally, which of the following *isn't* deadly to vampires?

   A. Wild roses
   B. Wooden stakes
   C. Garlic
   D. Silver bullets

5. Whose first acting job was in a Clearasil commercial?

   A. David Boreanaz
   B. Charisma Carpenter
   C. Sarah Michelle Gellar
   D. Alyson Hannigan

43

tainly appear that any future she and Angel could craft would have to involve finding a way to get rid of his demon once and for all. Not an easy task if the literary references are any indication. Dozens of ways to kill vampires have already passed into folklore, but to date, only one *cure* for vampirism has ever been seriously discussed: Killing the Master or the vampire's sire, enjoys some small notoriety in Eastern Europe as a way to free his "children." As Buffy has already slain the acknowledged Master, and Angel himself rather deftly inserted a crossbow bolt into Darla (Angel's sire despite her gender), and there has been no obvious benefit from either act, it seems that particular cure doesn't exist in Sunnydale. The arrival of Spike and Dru, whose joint and singular purpose was to restore Drusilla—by killing her sire, Angel, in the process—put the final nail in that theoretical coffin.

The notion of demonic possession causing vampirism isn't completely new. Like witches, vampires were sometimes held to be instruments of the devil, controlled by a demon placed inside the victim's body. The possession theory presents both hope and danger for Angel. Hope exists because what has been possessed may well be exorcised by the usual methods: the Catholic Church favors a ritual of prayer and the presence of holy artifacts. Christianity in general actually has a long history of exorcism on which to draw, with some well-developed rites to depossess the afflicted person.

---

## Everything I Ever Needed to Know, I Learned from *Buffy*

† Free trade is bad for fashion.

† Having a boyfriend who can fly makes it hard
to hide your diary.

† If your daughter has *two* history tutors, and the
principal is still calling, something's up.

† Never share a window ledge with the guy
who bit your mother.

**From beginning to ashy end, Darla just *loved* a good catfight.**

ANSWERS

1. C

2. D

3. D

4. D

5. A

The danger lies in figuring out what would be left once the demon vanished. Giles tells Buffy, "A vampire isn't a person at all. It may have the movements, the memories, even the personality of the person it took over, but it's still a demon at the core. There is no halfway." There is a strong indication that without his demon to animate him, there would be no Angel, just a vegetative lump that might not even survive.

Angel, however, has a different take on his situation. "The elders conjured up the perfect punishment for me: They restored my soul." Hmmm, does that mean Angel's soul is living cheek by jowl with his demon? What an interesting scenario! Maybe some form

## Written on the Wall

**Double-duty windows:** Alleys are either remarkably uniform in Sunnydale or . . . round? Keep an eye on the background as Buffy heads home from The Bronze. See that brilliant green window? Later, after an encounter with The Three, the Master's hired assassins, Buffy and Angel continue on toward Buffy's house—past the same window! Apparently, Buffy's house is located at *both* ends of the same lane.

\* \* \*

What exactly inspired Giles to bury himself in the library from "midnight until six"? Last we checked, Buffy didn't have a cell phone in her pocket, did she? So, when did she call him? For that matter, how did Darla know Angel had Buffy's place penciled into his diary for precisely that time? Or was she just making it all up as she went along?

\* \* \*

Buffy seems perfectly serious when she says, "Angel, do you snore?" Hasn't she noticed that he doesn't *breathe*?

\* \* \*

of exorcism just might be in order here—if he actually wanted to give up his vampiric ways.

Good vampires, while certainly a rarity, do exist in a number of novels and plays. One of the best known, St. Germaine, a character created by Chelsea Quinn Yarbo, was three thousand years old, and in all that time, he appears to have been relatively content with a lifestyle that allowed him considerable range as a scholar, that let him befriend incredible women, and that ensured he wouldn't die anytime soon. Inconveniences abounded, but he wasn't bothered by religious icons and certainly didn't spend those three thousand years looking for a way to cure himself!

Perhaps, as Willow suggested, Buffy and Angel might continue on exactly as they have been, with her getting older, and eventually, wrinkled, while Angel stayed young, dark, and handsome. Not a great solution.

All might not be completely hopeless though. Giles is happiest buried up to his chin in old books; perhaps, if it was strongly suggested to him, he might start looking for ways to save a vampire instead of stake one. Willow is jacked in to all the right resources—and, unlike Giles, she *likes* Angel. Who knows what she might turn up? Actually there was one other TV vampire who managed to become human again: Nick Knight's longtime paramour, the beautiful Janette. Through the simple, patient love of a human, she eventually found her way out of the darkness. Pity she was murdered just a few days later. . . .

Even if the answer isn't immediately apparent, viewers will likely forgive the romantic story line that's invading their perfectly good romp. We have a soft spot for young lovers, even when one of the lovers *is* two hundred and forty-one years old! When not taken to soap opera-ish excess, the impossible love affair has proven as enduring a theme as the vampire scenario itself.

**Even if Angel is more Irish than his accent suggests, he'd still have trouble with this Celtic beauty.**

**Betcha Buffy is questioning Willow's choice in men!**

# "I, Robot—You, Jane"

Everyone deserves a little romance in their lives, so there's really no reason why Buffy should object to Willow's newest boyfriend, right? Except . . . no one's ever seen him, not even Willow! . . . And he knows things about Buffy that only those who regularly break into her school records could know. . . . And, just as Willow's online romance heats up, her classmate decides to hang himself in the computer room. . . . And, well, there's the fact that a demon named Moloch has just escaped from one of Giles's old books and into Willow's favorite hangout, Sunnydale's computer network. Uh-oh.

the short version

## Away from the Cauldron and on to the Internet

**Rupert:** *What are you, a witch?*
**Jenny:** *. . . I don't have that kind of power. . . . I'm a technopagan.*

Witchcraft has come a long way since Shakespeare's witches intoned the "boil and bubble" speech in the middle of a Scottish moor. The good Bard certainly wouldn't recognize Jenny Calendar, who dangles a corkscrew from an unmentionable body part, as a witch! The witch trials ended, for the most

the longer look

49

## QUESTIONS

1. Which *Buffy the Vampire Slayer* regular studied tae kwon do for five years?

   A. Alyson Hannigan
   B. Charisma Carpenter
   C. Sarah Michelle Gellar
   D. Robia La Morte

2. Who *isn't* a historical demon?

   A. Baal
   B. Angelus
   C. Moloch
   D. Astaroth

3. Which actor played a robot for an episode of *Buffy the Vampire Slayer*?

   A. James Marsters
   B. Anthony Stewart Head
   C. Donald Sutherland
   D. John Ritter

4. What is Sarah Michelle Gellar's natural hair color?

   A. Blond
   B. Brunette
   C. Red
   D. Black

5. Which *Buffy the Vampire Slayer* regular played Lucy in *Dead Man on Campus*?

   A. Sarah Michelle Gellar
   B. Alyson Hannigan
   C. Charisma Carpenter
   D. Robia La Morte

## Who Was That?

EPISODE PRODUCTION NUMBER: 4V08
ORIGINAL AIR DATE: APRIL 28, 1997
WRITTEN BY: ASHLEY GABLE AND THOMAS A. SWYDEN
DIRECTED BY: STEPHEN POSEY

### CAST

| | |
|---|---|
| Buffy Summers | Sarah Michelle Gellar |
| Xander Harris | Nicholas Brendon |
| Willow Rosenberg | Alyson Hannigan |
| Rupert Giles | Anthony Stewart Head |

### GUEST CAST

| | |
|---|---|
| Ms. Jenny Calendar | Robia La Morte |
| Dave | Chad Lindberg |
| Fritz | Jamison Ryan |
| Thelonius | Pierrino Mascarino |
| School Nurse | Edith Fields |
| Male Student | Damon Sharp |
| Voice of Moloch | Mark Deakins |

part, in the 1700s. In 1951, Great Britain repealed its oppressive Witchcraft Laws. In 1990, the Internet began slinking its way into the average person's home. For the first time, isolated individuals whose interests tended toward so-called occult practices instead of the more traditional religions and lifestyles had a forum for sharing their calling, and the "technopagan" was born!

Just as many Christians find any discussion of witchcraft, broadly defined as an attempt to alter the environment by force of will, "too New Age," many pagans find this dabbling in the technical realm a step beyond their own wants or needs. Believing in witchcraft as an elemental Earth religion, Goddess worship, or even ceremonial magic, some see computers as one more way that modern civilizations are distancing themselves from the very forces of nature they've been striving to comprehend. The notion of sitting under artificial lights, in front of a mechanical box that beeps and whirs and probably throws out some sort of radiation, without a hint of human contact is, frankly, abhorrent to many pagans.

Most surprisingly, however, a considerable number of pagans are attracted to the energy and flow of computer systems. Many are systems operators, Web-page authors, engineers, and programmers. "It's all headwork, ya know?" says Clare Bonn. A self-proclaimed technopagan for more than seven years, Clare's day job features high-powered meetings among representatives of Canada's largest utilities and long hours spent organizing and improving her own utility's Internet and information services. "For me, a lot of magical practice involves meditation and visualization. If I invoke the four magical quarters, I picture guardian angels standing there. When I cast a protective circle, it's as real in my visualization as it is on the metaphysical planes. Computers are like that, too. You have to 'see' what's going on inside, be able to think in a certain way. Witches

## Everything I Ever Needed to Know, I Learned from *Buffy*

 † Even in Sunnydale, the shower is a dangerous place.

 † The TV is the idiot box; the computer is the "good box."

 † High School Rule #1: No secrets between
   people who've shared clothes.

 † Never use pop-culture references with a
   man who "skins" documents.

 † If your clique's dates include vampires, giant
 praying mantises, and demonically possessed computers,
   it's time to consider celibacy.

**ANSWERS**

**1. C**

**2. B**

**3. D**

**4. B**

**5. B**

**Okay, so Willow didn't get the guy—this time—at least she doesn't have Buffy's sort of clutter in her footlocker, either!**

call that sort of thinking a 'spell'; technopagans see patterns in programs as well. It really doesn't matter to me if I cast a circle on the ground or draw one on a screen because that's not where the real work is going on, that's all in my head and my soul. The outer circle is just symbolic." Jenny Calendar's magical workspace, the spiritual circle designed to capture Moloch the Corruptor, worked on the same principles, as Jenny surrounded her high-tech computer terminal with real beeswax candles that would do traditional witches proud.

Therese Thibideau, one of Clare's far-flung friends, found a whole new world opening to her once the Internet came to her tiny community in the Northwest Territories. "I know there are thousands of solitary practitioners out there, who actually prefer to work alone, but I'm not one of them, and even finding another pagan, much less one working in my tradition, in a community of less than five hundred people was . . . impossible." Simple isolation has prompted many pagans and witches to turn to a wider, if different, community online. "It was so satisfying to be part of group celebrations again, to feel connected." So far Therese's circle includes practitioners in Prague, York, Brussels, tiny six hundred–person Tlingit in New Zealand, and, coincidentally, one in *Sunnyvale*, California.

Even pagans in large centers have been turning to the Net and the computer bulletin boards linked to it. Claude Bellenger, who lives in Montreal and is already part of a close-knit coven, had a completely different reason for blending magic and technology. "It's only recently that a forum for truly free speech has arisen. On the Internet, we can educate a public whose only other exposure to pagans has been those sensationalized bits aired on Halloween. For some reason, those agencies never notice the witches who *don't* like to sleep in coffins, the pagans who *don't* paint their windows black to avoid the sun, the normal people out there who simply follow a different religious path."

He knows that changing public opinion takes time and patience, which probably explains his calm when a major online service summarily removed his personal Web page when another subscriber complained that the company was fostering "Satanism and violence." "The company yanked the page without even reading it. When I pushed for a review, they realized the page was a positive, historically relevant piece that advocated peaceful resolution of religious differences. The page went back up, with a public apology by the company for its temporary unavailability. It's always frustrating to deal with prejudice and ignorance, but in the long run, the page did exactly what it was designed to do: educate."

If neopagans had cause to cry foul after "The Witch," claiming *Buffy* had fallen prey to stereotypes, and as one fan claimed, "was content to write meaningless stories without any background, without any research," "I, Robot—You, Jane" did exactly what Claude Bellenger proposed the new technologies should do—it educated. Says Bellenger, "Though I've never personally chased a demon off the Internet, the portrayal of a technopagan was balls-

## Written on the Wall

The records Moloch opens in his quest to get rid of Buffy contain some fascinating, if contradictory, information. Buffy's birthday, previously given as October 24, 1980, is listed here as May 6, 1979. Instead of being a senior, as in the movie, she's a sophomore. Then again, with a grade point average of 2.8, Buffy could stay a sophomore long enough for Willow, and even Xander, to graduate!

\* \* \*

Any number of shows have included cameos by their creators. Alfred Hitchcock, the grand old gentleman of horror, was famous for clever appearances in many of his films. Just last year, Chris Carter, creator of *The X-Files,* spent a few minutes on-screen. Joss Whedon chose a little more subtle way of becoming part of his show by supplying his voice for the radio announcer heard in the background.

\* \* \*

on accurate! Jenny Calendar is a terrific character, and, without doubt, will remain a fan favorite while the two-dimensional Amy fades."

Even pagans who would normally consider themselves artists rather than technicians dabble in cyberspace's surf. Gail Peitsch, whose work adorns dozens of public buildings in Canada and Great Britain, never thought she'd find a use for the computer her husband bought literally "for a song." It didn't have a lot of bells and whistles, but it did have a modem, a color printer, and some basic Web/image publishing programs. Within days, Gail produced her first three-dimensional design. "Moonrise" sold for nearly a quarter of a million dollars when a gallery owner, impressed with the production process, decided to sell the piece through an online auction.

"I'd heard of chat rooms," Gail says. "I wasn't totally out of the loop, but I'd never realized how 'normal' the chatters were. Movies and talk shows portrayed them as places where sexual perverts liked to hang out. I didn't find that at all. It'd been some time since I'd been to a large gathering of any type, pagan or artistic, and it was so refreshing to listen to people from such different backgrounds come together to discuss common interests. My only problem was that, being an artist, I wasn't really satisfied with seeing nothing but words scroll across the scene. The very first time I attended an online pagan celebration, I started thinking, 'You know, with some good art, this could be a beautiful place to get together.'"

Gail's basic plan—echoed onscreen in "I, Robot—You Jane" as Jenny built her circle of technopagans—was to create a computer environment, which could be manipulated by a number of participants. Sounds like a good game, but it's more than that. The first room she created naturally reflected her interest in things pagan, and included all the ingredients required to celebrate in her own tradition. Each person who called into the program could also manipulate all the items. As she explained, "We were physically separate, but through the computer, we worked together to a common goal. The goal just happened to have a pagan focus."

The process has since been given to a number of task-management programmers who are wowed by the sophistication of Gail's creation. "It's the smoothest interface we've ever seen for multitasking. It's simple, elegant, easy to adapt. What more could we want?" asks Creativity Labs' Alex Balwin.

Those who call themselves practicing technopagans also applaud the work. "We've been blending other philosophies for centuries, why not these two?" asks Claude Bellenger. "The world of cyberspace is very like the human mind. It forms connections in response to need, it actively adapts to new information, and it recognizes the gaps in its knowledge base. We hope that linking pagan thinking, pagan priorities, and pagan philosophy will, ultimately, create an environment that fosters both magic and technology, an environment that sees the value of both."

Jenny Calendar would be satisfied if Rupert could tell the TV from the computer monitor!

**Even the nonvampiric-type demons have a thing for Buffy's neck!**

# "The Puppet Show"

As Sunnydale High prepares to dazzle an audience of bored classmates and the obligatory gaggle of teachers and parents at the annual "Talentless Show," Buffy juggles her demanding one-line role in *Oedipus Rex* and a hunt for an organ-snatching demon whose taste in "donors" extends to students and staff alike. The fact that an unlikely demon-hunter can't seem to separate Buffy from the demons isn't making her show-business career any easier!

## Hunting Demons

Demons hold every longevity record in the things-that-go-bump-in-the-night category. They're everywhere. Even Sunnydale's mythology incorporates demonology into its own unique story line by making demons the primary, in fact the only, cause of vampirism! Without demons, there'd be no vampires to stake, no strange entities to take over Giles's girlfriend, and Angel, well, Angel would really have been buried in Ireland nearly two hundred years ago! Demons exist in Judaic theology, Christian scripture, Islamic texts, Hindu folktales. . . . Well, let's just say the list of religions that don't include descriptions of demons in their literature is a lot shorter than the list of faiths that *do.*

## QUESTIONS

1. Who was born in Camdentown, England?

   A. Anthony Stewart Head
   B. James Marsters
   C. Juliet Landau
   D. Julie Benz

2. Which of the following films *haven't* featured animated dolls?

   A. *Child's Play*
   B. *The Puppet Master*
   C. *Leprechaun*
   D. *Cat's Eye*

3. Who portrayed characters on *Deep Space Nine* and *Buffy the Vampire Slayer* simultaneously?

   A. David Boreanaz
   B. Armin Shimerman
   C. Anthony Stewart Head
   D. Seth Green

4. Whose real-life appearance in his summer camp's talent show performance of *Hello, Dolly* at age six started him on the road to a successful acting career?

   A. David Boreanaz
   B. Armin Shimerman
   C. Anthony Stewart Head
   D. Seth Green

# Who Was That?

**EPISODE PRODUCTION NUMBER:** 4V09
**ORIGINAL AIR DATE:** MAY 5, 1997
**WRITTEN BY:** DEAN BATALI AND ROB DES HOTEL
**DIRECTED BY:** ELLEN PRESSMAN

## CAST

| | |
|---|---|
| Buffy Summers | Sarah Michelle Gellar |
| Xander Harris | Nicholas Brendon |
| Willow Rosenberg | Alyson Hannigan |
| Cordelia Chase | Charisma Carpenter |
| Rupert Giles | Anthony Stewart Head |

## GUEST CAST

| | |
|---|---|
| Mrs. Joyce Summers | Kristine Sutherland |
| Morgan | Richard Werner |
| Marc | Burke Roberts |
| Principal Snyder | Armin Shimerman |
| Mrs. Jackson | Lenora May |
| Elliot | Chasen Hampton |
| Lisa | Natasha Pearce |
| Voice of Sid | Tom Wyner |
| Emily | Krissy Carlson |
| Locker Girl | Michelle Miracle |

Oddly enough, considering the pervasiveness of their occupancy in fable and legend as well as in religious mythology, relatively little folklore suggests any effective ways to destroy them! Traditional vampires come with built-in weaknesses to garlic cloves, sunlight, and holy water. Werewolves—even in Sunnydale—remain severely allergic to silver bullets and wolfsbane. Biblical passages and crowfoot really tick off leprechauns, and, if you believe the legends, running water makes magicians more than a little seasick. Demons, however, are susceptible to only three known methods of complete and irrevocable destruction. Pity it appears that neither Sid, Sunnydale's visiting demon-hunter, nor Buffy had read *The Demon Slayer's Handbook*—it would have made their job tons easier.

Being incorporeal, as most demons are believed to be, automatically eliminates some of Buffy's favorite means of disposal. Repeatedly staking a traditional demon might make your arm sore, but it will do diddly-squat to the demon. Decapitation poses similar problems, and, with nothing physically present to splash it *on*, all the holy water in all the churches in the Old World isn't going to banish any demons. Demon-hunters, unlike their vampire- and werewolf-hunting kin, can travel light, leaving all the stakes, bullets, and crosses at home. If the demon doesn't simply devour them right away, demon-hunters can depend on a memorized liturgy of spells and incantations, maybe a bit of incense, and a piece of chalk. Of course, having a list of demon names doesn't hurt, either, but more on that later.

Although Buffyverse demons tend to turn up incarnate, in some body, be it undead, regularly dead, or the current home of some living person, traditional demons are more likely to show up as windstorms, billowing smoke, blasts of heat, or, if they are really ticked, as firestorms. Still, demonic possession isn't limited to Sunnydale, and what works on the ghostly demon usually works on the body-snatching variety, too.

Though *demon* once referred to the "heathen" kings surrounding ancient Judaic communities, its current meaning has shifted somewhat, describing an anti-angel of sorts. The war in heaven, which the angel Michael supposedly won when Lucifer fell, formalized the idea of angelic and demonic ranks. Angels gained obtuse titles such as "powers," "principalities," "thrones," "dominions," "cherubs," "seraphim," and the regular "angels." Demons, which centuries of theologians have determined may have originally been the seraphim, for some reason took on much more human titles:

5. **Which *Buffy the Vampire Slayer* regular was a San Diego Chargers cheerleader?**

   A. Alyson Hannigan
   B. Robia La Morte
   C. Sarah Michelle Gellar
   D. Charisma Carpenter

59

**ANSWERS**

1. A

2. C

3. B

4. D

5. D

**If the talent show was held in graveyards,
or libraries, or the backseats of expensive convertibles,
this bunch would be shoe-ins!**

"demon-kings," "demon-princes," "demon-barons," even "demon-presidents." (Hmmm, that last one explains a lot!)

The first step in the demon-destruction process is simply determining who it is you're trying to get rid of. If all the demon-hunters who came before Sid knew their business, all Sid and Buffy needed to do to prevent their demon from hustling body parts backstage was to surround him and call him by his title and his name. Since Sid knew he was dealing with the last of his seven demons, he must have had some information to use against them, and some idea who

## Everything I Ever Needed to Know, I Learned from *Buffy*

✝ Sometimes there really *is* something under the bed!

✝ Never stand under a chandelier while
hunting demons or dummies.

✝ Never help a demon demonstrate his equipment—
on your head!

✝ Given a choice between detention and a
talent-show appearance, choose detention!

✝ Smoking may be a leading cause of cancer-related deaths,
but it's "woolly-headed liberal thinking" that gets you
eaten by cannibals.

✝ The best way for a parent to support their child's scholastic
efforts is to stay away from the school—especially events such as
Parent-Teacher Nights and talent shows.

✝ If demons regularly steal brains at your school,
a low grade-point average isn't necessarily a
life-threatening disadvantage, right?

he was chasing. A name would guarantee that the demon-hunter's expulsion would be effective, but simply identifying the demon's rank, and commanding it by invoking the name of a higher-ranked demon to leave his victim, should have allowed Sid to force this last demon from its host body temporarily. Once out of the host body, and a little holy scripture and chanting later, the demon could be sent back to its life in Hell. Of course, Sid was a puppet, so maybe he'd have had trouble wrapping his wooden jaw around names like Kasdeya, Belphegor, or Amduscias.

If Sid and Buffy were simply trying to shift this particular demon off the Hellmouth, however, they could do that without getting on intimate, first-name terms with it. Demons, like those

# Written on the Wall

Oops. It's just awful to spoil a heart-wrenching—not to mention heart-stabbing—scene with a blooper, but that's exactly what happened as poor Sid sacrificed himself to destroy the last of the demons of the Brotherhood of Seven. As a scene, it was a real tearjerker—if you weren't too busy looking for the disappearing knife! One second, it's just sort of sticking out of the demon's chest; the next, as Buffy picks up the lifeless remains of Sid, it has mysteriously disappeared.

\* \* \*

More bloopers. Keeping track of Willow's efforts at the computer was more difficult than usual this episode. In one scene, the sound of Willow's fingers clicking across the keys continues long after her hands leave the keyboard. Moments later, though she's working away, absolutely *nothing* is happening on the screen of the monitor supposedly connected to her terminal!

\* \* \*

poor souls who, even though allergic to chocolate, simply can't pass it up, are attracted to the very things that hurt them. Biblical or Talmudic phrases, scattered like breadcrumbs to another location, will draw the demon along their path as it seeks to devour the bits of paper and, hopefully, find the sacred book and destroy that as well. To prevent the demon from returning requires just the skills for which Buffy is so rightly infamous. No demon willingly returns to a scene where one of its kind, and in the Buffyverse that would include vampires, died. With the exception of Angel's, Buffy has no qualms about providing vampire ashes.

For a more permanent exit, demon-hunters had only one option, the dissolution of the demonic spirit itself, and to that end, the whole bell-book-and-candle routine was whipped out—or in this case, the book-saltwater-and-blade routine. After catching its attention by calling out its name and rank, then either ejecting it from its host body or luring the host to a suitable location, the demon-hunter contained his prey by chanting without break from a holy text. With the demon entranced (or pissed off as the case might be), it was sprayed with salt water, which reputedly begins breaking down the body. Once the demon is flushed free, again an amorphous being, it's vulnerable on an entirely different plane. A sacred knife (some say the predecessor of the ceremonial blade used by modern Wiccans), its blade covered in runic representations of the demon's name, can, with a single stroke, scatter demonic souls like motes of dust!

Much less messy than the dramatic scene facing the audience of the Sunnydale High Annual Talentless Show.

And something to remember for the next time Buffy fights a demon.

And, like, you just *know* there's going to be a next time, right?

Definitely *not* every sixteen-year-old's idea of a "dream" man!

# EPISODE:
## "Nightmares"

the short version

Reality redshifts into the twilight zone when dreams, stray thoughts, and, with increasing frequency, nightmares start taking on real forms inside Sunnydale's town limits. The Master may still be locked inside his lair, but his spirit is busy on the commute, as is the astral projection of an unconscious young boy who is rapidly becoming the only constant in Buffy's distorted world. Realigning reality may well depend on finding a way to lure this boy from the safety of his unconsciousness, but how can she do that if her own worst nightmare, that she'll become a vampire herself, comes true?

## I Spy with My Sleeping Eye

the longer look

At first glance, "Nightmares" is just another *Buffy* episode, another case of monsters in the basement and the odd vampire popping up at inconvenient moments, but in fact, among the thirty-plus episodes to air in the show's first season, "Nightmares" is quite unique. Instead of featuring an apparently normal situation that turns out to have been fraught with distinctly paranormal dangers, "Nightmares" begins as a blatantly paranormal situation that is actually grounded in an all-too-human form of horror. Instead of apparently normal

## QUESTIONS

1. Which of the following
films *didn't* feature a vampire?

   A. *Nightmare Castle*
   B. *Nightmare on Elm Street*
   C. *Nightmare in Blood*
   D. *Nightmare Lake*

2. Which of the following is
not a dream-time mon-
ster?

   A. Mara
   B. Hag
   C. Incubus
   D. Ghoul

3. Which of these *Buffy the
Vampire Slayer* regulars
hasn't been required to
appear without their usual
street clothes?

   A. Sarah Michelle Gellar
   B. Seth Green
   C. Alyson Hannigan
   D. Nicholas Brendon

4. Which occasional *Buffy
the Vampire Slayer* partici-
pant appeared in the 1971
gore-fest *Vampire Circus*?

   A. James Marsters
   B. Ken Lerner
   C. Mark Metcalf
   D. Robin Sachs

# Who Was That?

EPISODE PRODUCTION NUMBER: 4V10
ORIGINAL AIR DATE: MAY 12, 1997
STORY WRITTEN BY: JOSS WHEDON
TELEPLAY WRITTEN BY: DAVID GREENWALT
DIRECTED BY: BRUCE SETH GREEN

## CAST

| | |
|---|---|
| Buffy Summers | Sarah Michelle Gellar |
| Xander Harris | Nicholas Brendon |
| Willow Rosenberg | Alyson Hannigan |
| Rupert Giles | Anthony Stewart Head |

## GUEST CAST

| | |
|---|---|
| The Master | Mark Metcalf |
| Mrs. Joyce Summers | Kristine Sutherland |
| Billy Palmer | Jeremy Foley |
| Collin/The Anointed | Andrew J. Ferchland |
| Hank Summers | Dean Butler |
| Wendell | Justin Urich |
| Laura | J. Robin Miller |
| Ms. Tishler | Terry Cain |
| Aldo Gianfranco | Scott Harlan |
| Coach | Brian Pietro |
| Way Cool Guy | Johnny Green |
| Cool Guy's Mom | Patty Ross |
| Doctor | Dom Magwili |
| Stage Manager | Sean Moran |

teachers who turn into giant bugs, or cosmetics salesmen who turn into little bugs, or even classmates who turn into werewolves, "Nightmares" featured a "monster in the basement" who coached Little League!

In a community whose biggest tourist attraction seems to be a mystical Hellmouth, you'd almost expect its citizens' nightmares to feature the most exotic of phobias. Instead, Willow faces stage fright, and Xander is haunted by a childhood encounter with a clown. Even Buffy's fear isn't of the vampires themselves, but of losing her humanity. And, when Billy Palmer's fears finally find expression, the requisite paranormal element is firmly rooted in the human psyche.

One in twenty real-world people have reported an out-of-body experience of some type. The NDE (near-death experience) of the desperately ill or injured, complete with the dark tunnel, the bright light, and, for some, the enchanting Otherwhere, which has been described as a renewed Garden of Eden, is reported once or twice a month at Mount Sinai Hospital. A chaplain at Lutheran Memorial recalls one particularly busy week when twelve patients required his "If you believe in an afterlife . . . or if you prefer to think of these experiences as a succession of small neural flashes in an overstressed brain . . ." speech. Father Rowney, one of four chaplains serving the Greater Islands Health Sciences Centre, figures he spends between twenty-five to thirty hours a month helping patients come to terms with an experience "they feel defies all the laws of their physical world. Billy Palmer is obviously a fictional character, but stripped of its made-for-TV drama, the essential elements of his experience do have real-world parallels. Billy Palmer felt severe physical and emotional disassociation. He 'returned' from the experience with a new strength, a new willingness to confront problems head-on. Billy Palmer's metaphysical excursions centered around a key figure in his life. In other words, despite the fact none of our patients reappear to their families with a 'bad man' in tow, all the essential parts of a near-death experience are certainly elements of the 'Nightmares' script. From what I've seen, *Buffy* plays on that interesting edge between what we know and what we fear, the perfect plot-line fodder."

5. **Which two *Buffy the Vampire Slayer* regulars discuss Philly cheesesteak with considerable expertise?**

A. Anthony Stewart Head
B. Nicholas Brendon
C. David Boreanaz
D. Seth Green

**ANSWERS**

**1. B**

**2. D**

**3. C**

**4. D**

**5. C and D**

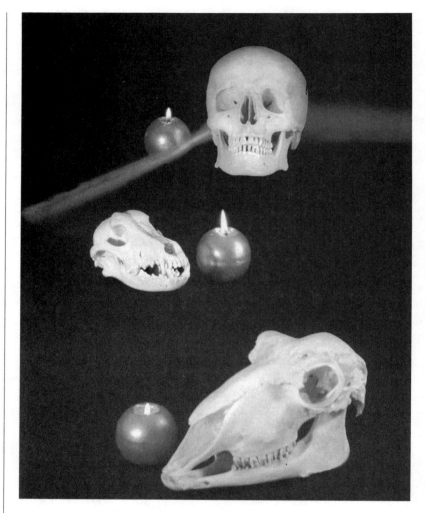

**Sometimes fear is all in your head.**

Of course, not all patients experience what Father Rowney jokingly refers to as "the full Monty." "Many more people report a sort of displaced consciousness," he explains. "It's the hovering-over-the-bed sensation that allows them to look down on themselves as doctors and nurses go about their business. We know, from the multitude of monitors common in trauma rooms, that patients who experience these events are technically unconscious. A woman I recently counseled arrived in our ER with skull trauma so severe, we really felt her situation was hopeless. The staff worked as hard on her as they had on anyone, but one of the nurses, seeing a Catholic medal among the woman's personal effects, had already called me.

"When I arrived, she was in full cardiac and respiratory arrest; her blood pressure was almost undetectable. Frankly, she was closer to dead than alive. Her brain-wave functions were so depressed that, if they hadn't known I was on my way, they would probably have aborted life-sustaining efforts.

"Now, I'd like to think that it was my arrival that sparked something, but to be honest, miracles come more often from the hands of well-trained medical staffs than they do from me." Father Rowney's chuckle is rich, without the slightest hint of reverence. "She didn't regain consciousness during my brief time in the emergency room, but her heart rate evened out, and she began breathing on her own. I was there for no more than a few minutes, and as I was leaving, one of the nurses called out, 'That's one for our side, eh, Father?'

"I didn't see [the patient] again for over a week. She remained unconscious and was kept in our ICU during that time. No one except her daughter and husband, and their family priest, was even allowed near her. There was no way she could have heard about my appearance. But the day she was brought into the general ward, she recognized me immediately! She described our brief encounter in precise detail—right down to the ER nurse's scorekeeping. It

---

## Everything I Ever Needed to Know, I Learned from *Buffy*

† Letting a deep-seated fear of clowns fester
can cause psychological problems later in life—
not to mention sore knuckles.

† You know you're in love when the center of your
universe suddenly resembles your worst nightmare, and you'd
still meet her under the bleachers.

† Smoking in school just ain't worth it.

## Written on the Wall

Willow keeps the most interesting things inside her locker! Last week, it was a picture of everyone's favorite librarian. This week, there's a Nerf Herder bumper sticker adorning her door. Nerf Herder, of course, has a particular link to *Buffy the Vampire Slayer*. They're the band responsible for the show's wake-up-and-take-notice theme song.

\* \* \*

Oops. Okay, so it was a nightmare sequence, but how exactly did Buffy *the vampire* get to the hospital? It was, after all, daylight outside the spooky new cemetery that defied all physical laws.

\* \* \*

Willow must have two too many backpacks for her own good. Watch this episode closely, and you'll see her take the same backpack off twice—without putting it back on in between!

\* \* \*

shocked me. I can only imagine how inexplicable it must have seemed to her."

In choosing a vehicle for their story line, *Buffy*'s crew dug deeply into what is perhaps one of the few *human* mysteries remaining.

The mere fact that such NDE cases aren't front-page news says a great deal about their frequency and their universality. Donna Rich, the Coordinator of Nursing Studies at Brightham Medical College, shrugs off such incidents. "I don't know many nurses who *don't* have similar stories. In fact, we include a practical response to such experiences in our training course. Just as we brief our staff on the traditional handling of the dead in a variety of cultures—for example, certain Judaic rituals require the family's attention before we can send a body for postmortem exam—we also detail a variety of responses to these out-of-body or near-death experiences and encourage our nurses to be open-minded should a patient wish to discuss such an event. It's also standard teaching practice to remind our nurses that 'unconscious' patients *do* seem to be more aware than we'd credit."

Rich's suggested responses are indeed varied: "Some patients regard it [the NDE] as a religious revelation, and if that is their belief, then we treat it as such and call in our chaplain. If the patient is frightened and seems inclined to want a rational explanation, then there are medical conditions which can account for many of the sensations common to these experiences. For example, if you've ever fainted and watched your vision tunnel as the floor reached up to slap you, you've likely experienced the 'traveling down a long tunnel' part of the event. The brilliant light at the end *may* also be caused by oxygen deprivation. Divers sometimes report similar symptoms if their tanks aren't perfectly clean. Then there's the patient who sees this 'astral projection' as a psychic event; they want a different type of explanation." She smiles. "Usually they want to know if they can 'do it again.' They seem to think of the whole thing as a sort of mental roller coaster with an endorphin high at the end of the ride. I'm not trying to belittle anyone's experience here, but the responses are all quite different, everything from sincere fear to euphoria. I don't know exactly what these patients feel or experience—it's never happened to me—but I imagine that, in a sense, it doesn't matter if it's 'real.' The effects on the patient most certainly are."

The rarest of the out-of-body experiences is the one featured in "Nightmares." It's actually a combination of two separate types of so-called psychic phenomena. The first part, the projection, is, as noted earlier, not all that uncommon among the very ill. It's the second part, generally called "apparition"—the ability of a second individual, unconnected to the first, to recognize the projection's appearance—that's truly wiggy. Yet it, too, has been reliably recorded within real-world experience.

Joanne Hart of London fell from a third-floor landing in her home at about 9:35 A.M. Joanne heard the grandfather clock chime the half hour just before tripping over her son, Jeremy's, prized roller skates, which were left lying in the hallway. Joanne lay unconscious for more than an hour. During that time her cousin, Didi

Ford, who was some forty minutes across town, "saw" Joanne fall, "saw" her lying crumpled on the rug in the waiting room of the doctor for whom Didi worked, and "saw" blood seep from the corner of her slack mouth. "It was so real. I actually stood up to go touch her." Three years later, Ms. Ford is still shaking her head when she discusses the incident that nearly convinced her employer that his receptionist had gone mad. "I called out to him to come quick because someone was hurt, then headed around the desk to see what I could do. It happened so quickly that I actually thought a patient had come in while I was looking down, [and had] tripped and fallen in the waiting room! It wasn't until I stood up that I realized it was Jo—and that it couldn't be Jo in the middle of our office."

Didi Ford's embarrassment as she relates the events of that morning is clear. "I didn't really realize that I wasn't seeing a real person, I mean a person who was really there, until she . . . well, she disappeared. I was left half-crouched over the rug in front of my desk, with my boss and two of his patients just staring at me."

Didi didn't see any background imagery at all. "It was as if she just walked in. I couldn't picture her at home, at the club, at the grocery store, nothing." Though she was anxious to put the incident behind her, she waited until both patients had left the waiting room before she called her cousin's house at 10:25. Not getting an answer, she rang Joanne's husband at his office and he, knowing Joanne had every intention of staying home that morning, also tried to reach her. When there was still no answer, he called the neighbor and asked her to check in on his wife. According to Emergency Services, the neighbor's call for an ambulance came in at 10:42.

When Joanne regained her senses just before supper that same day, her first groggy request was to see Didi.

EPISODE:

# "Invisible Girl," a.k.a. "Out of Sight, Out of Mind"

**A** series of deliberate "accidents" is suddenly plaguing Sunnydale High and, except for Angel, there isn't a vampire in sight! First Cordelia's boyfriend is clobbered by an invisible assailant; then Cordelia's best friend is shoved down a flight of stairs by an unseen enemy; then Cordelia's favorite teacher is attacked by a floating plastic bag. Suspecting that Cordelia is somehow the ultimate target, Buffy spends her time during the May Queen preparations following Cordy from dress fitting to dress fitting and trying to figure out how she can fight what she can't see!

> **the short version**

## All Hail the Queen of the May!

All teenagers live in the now, so it's hardly surprising that Cordelia Chase would desperately want to be May Queen without realizing that in addition to being the title for the winner of a high-school popularity contest and the name of a pretty good tune, *May Queen* is also a title for the honoree of a ritual that goes back hundreds of years. In fact, considering her opinion of last year's nail colors, she'd probably have boycotted the whole thing if the word *old* came up in the descriptions!

Certainly, customs like rolling about in the morning grass to soak yourself wouldn't instantly appeal to "Queen C"—not

> **the longer look**

73

**May Queen just isn't all it's cracked up to be.**

unless she'd heard that May 1, or May Day, dew was a veritable Fountain of Youth. May Day, coronation day for the May Queen, was, if modern neopagans have their calendars straight, Beltane, a pagan festival celebrating the birth of spring, the renewal of life, and fertility. Traditionally, young women hurried outside before the sun could rise and washed their faces with Beltane dew to capture the essence of youthful spring and stay freshly beautiful forever. Those with tons of people to gather dew for them—and presumably a bigger backyard—bathed in it to maintain a perky bustline, slender waist, and firm bottom. Now that might appeal to Cordelia.

So might the notion of having her own coterie of handmaids—and a few handmen, too—to satisfy her every whim as she was paraded through town, decked out in flowers and the best labels. A Yorkshire version of May Queen celebrations relates a tale of milkmaids parading through town with their milk pails in hand, calling out suggestive comments to all the men lining the streets, and flashing some ankle from beneath the hems of their skirts (and

# Who Was That?

EPISODE PRODUCTION NUMBER: 4V11

ORIGINAL AIR DATE: MAY 19, 1997

STORY WRITTEN BY: JOSS WHEDON

TELEPLAY WRITTEN BY: ASHLEY GABLE AND THOMAS A. SWYDEN

DIRECTED BY: REZA BADIYI

## CAST

| | |
|---|---|
| Buffy Summers | Sarah Michelle Gellar |
| Xander Harris | Nicholas Brendon |
| Willow Rosenberg | Alyson Hannigan |
| Cordelia Chase | Charisma Carpenter |
| Rupert Giles | Anthony Stewart Head |

## GUEST CAST

| | |
|---|---|
| Angel | David Boreanaz |
| Marcie Ross | Clea Duvall |
| Principal Snyder | Armin Shimerman |
| Mitch | Ryan Bittle |
| Ms. Miller | Denise Dowse |
| Bud 1 | John Knight |
| Harmony | Mercedes McNab |
| Agent Doyle | Mark Phelan |
| Agent Manetti | Skip Stellrecht |
| FBI Teacher | Julie Fulton |

1. **Which of the following film titles is fictitious?**

   A. *The Invisible Man*
   B. *The Invisible Woman*
   C. *Invisible Agent*
   D. *The Invisible Dog*

2. **Which *Buffy the Vampire Slayer* actress was born July 23?**

   A. Alyson Hannigan
   B. Charisma Carpenter
   C. Sarah Michelle Gellar
   D. Julie Benz

3. **In what year was the original *Buffy the Vampire Slayer* film released?**

   A. 1990
   B. 1992
   C. 1994
   D. 1996

4. **Traditionally, invisibility can be achieved by carrying any of the following, except:**

   A. The heart of a bat
   B. A drop of mercury
   C. A frog
   D. The comb of a black rooster

---

## Everything I Ever Needed to Know, I Learned from *Buffy*

† Baseball-bat damage is probably tough to airbrush out of May King photos.

† If your date, your favorite teacher, *and* your best friend all claim to have been attacked by an invisible assailant, paranoia is a pretty reasonable response.

† There really is a job for everyone, even invisible people.

---

sometimes more than ankle!) all in an effort to convince men to toss silver pennies into their pails! A beauty contest where the winners can *spend* the votes! Right up Cordelia's alley.

And, with Cordelia's love of leather seats and broom closets, she might even enjoy the May Queen's traditional role in blessing the spring fields. Making love under a starry sky amid spring's first flowers isn't every girl's romantic ideal, but it's got to beat scrambling around in Daddy's car with a stick shift jabbing your ribs, or a little sweater-yanking in a utility closet where the sweetest scents are mildewed mops and high-potency urinal cleansers!

Spending the entire evening publically pursued by the medieval equivalent of the football captain, being wooed with sweets and pretty ribbons, and being the central figure for every dance, could tweak Cordelia's interest, as could being carried through town on the shoulders of all the eligible young men!

So, where's the downside?

Well, also according to tradition, the May Queen ends up Kingless!

Instead of having a fairy-tale ending as did Cinderella or Sleeping Beauty, the May Queen's ardent lover, more likely known as the Green Man or Jack-in-the-Green than as the May King, is killed! Biggest night of the May Queen's year, everyone else out reveling in the bushes, and the May Queen ends up dateless! Not much of a deal from a modern point of view.

From a pagan perspective, this death merely paves the way for the Green Man to be reborn in a new incarnation and for summer's fertility to be fulfilled; the Green Man's blood seeps into the earth and ensures a bountiful growing season and harvest. Birth and death are closely intertwined, especially as seen in the context of

## Written on the Wall

Who says Angel has no prospects? True, his aspirations are different—he doesn't really want a window office after all—but there are possibilities. Take that "no breath" thing, for example: Bet the gas company could find just the perfect job for him—mostly underground, too!

\* \* \*

Oops, time continuity boo-boos continue. See the sign up on The Bronze's bulletin board? *Closed for Fumigation.* No sweat—except we've already seen the big postfumigation in the previous episode, "Angel." Even The Bronze shouldn't fumigate twice in two weeks!

\* \* \*

Hmmm . . . was Marcie wandering about Sunnydale High in her birthday suit?

\* \* \*

Either the prop people have a great sense of humor, or they just don't know anything about Infiltration and Assassination. Catch the text under the chapter title of Marcie's new schoolbook? Most of the page is pure gobbledygook, but a large section is devoted to the Beatles' "Happiness Is a Warm Gun."

\* \* \*

Seems the cast of *Buffy the Vampire Slayer* couldn't decide what to have for lunch during this episode. Watch the hands of anyone eating anything, and you'll see Xander's chips change into a sandwich, and back, while Buffy's french fries turn into sodas.

\* \* \*

5. Which supernatural creature doesn't, historically, have the ability to become invisible?

A. Ghost
B. Nighthag
C. Vampire
D. Werewolf

**ANSWERS**

1. D

2. B

3. B

4. B

5. D

the pagan religious calendar, which focuses on the agrarian lifestyle.

A celebration that has survived into the present in some areas, the Dancing of the Maypole, symbolizes many of the birth-death and male-female balances central to the pagan philosophy. The pole, like most taller-than-wide monuments, fits right into Freud's "phallic symbol" theory and is the masculine aspect of the celebration. The ribbons, usually carried by both men and women, are the feminine aspect which, wrapped around the Maypole at the end of the dancing, is said to symbolize the Goddess embracing the God.

Oh, yeah, the May Queen is an aspect of the Goddess. Wouldn't Cordelia's ego be flattered to know that she was a goddess, if only for a single day? Probably. Right up to the point where someone told her that the May Queen must, as the year progresses, inevitably become the Crone!

Maybe she's better off kept in the dark or not knowing.

# EPISODE:
# "Prophecy Girl"

**W**hen Buffy discovers that her Watcher has been holding out on her—little things like a major prophecy insisting the Master is about to rise and slay *her*!—Buffy goes ballistic. Like the Master couldn't pick a better time than in the middle of Spring Fling? It's too much for our Slayer and she promptly hands in her notice, a resignation her Watcher just can't accept. As the body count among her classmates begins to rise, Buffy is drawn inexorably back to her encounter with the mad vampire.

the short version

## The Good Guys

Though any number of characters leave us wondering just whose side they're on—Principal Snyder pops quickly to mind!—the Good Guys are the true blue, tried-and-true personas that tug on our heartstrings week after week, the ones that draw us into a world that, without the richly drawn "people," would appear ridiculous indeed!

the longer look

**Nicholas Brendon, the Saner Side of Xander Harris**
Though Xander Harris could easily have devolved into little more than Buffy's wisecracking puppy dog, the character, through the creativity of the *BTVS* writers and the work of a

## Performance Credits——Nicholas Brendon

**Commercial Credit**—Clearasil Spokesperson

**TV**—*Married . . . with Children* (1993)—Guy in Ray-Ray's Gang

**TV**—*Dave's World* (1994)

**TV**—*Secret Lives* (1995)—unaired pilot

**Stage**—*The Further Adventures of Tom Sawyer*

**Stage**—*My Own Private Hollywood*

**Stage**—*Out of Gas on Lover's Leap*

**Film**—*Children of the Corn III—Urban Harvest* (1994)—Basketball Player One

### Best Line as Xander

"I laugh in the face of danger. Then I hide till it goes away!"

talented young actor, remains an engaging, three-dimensional persona as capable of edgy, tension-filled conflicts as superbly timed pranks and comebacks.

Hard as it may be to believe, Nicholas Brendon, along with his twin brother Kelly, was born April 12, 1971—making him more than a decade older than the Xander Harris character he began playing in 1997! Just as age hasn't been a barrier to good acting, however, neither has genre in his career as a thespian.

### Alyson Hannigan Tones It Down to Play Willow Rosenberg

If Nicholas Brendon has a short acting history, Alyson Hannigan's, which began in 1979 when she was just *five*, more than balances things out. Anyone who follows her career quickly realizes how varied her roles have been—if you haven't, catch her in the R-rated film *Dead Man on Campus,* which was just released—but might have trouble identifying just which of her many qualities makes her appearances so memorable. Sure, she's got a cute nose, beautiful eyes, and a smile that could light up a coal mine, but it's less what she has that creates her characters than what she *does* with that incredibly mobile face. Like the golden-era actresses who realized how very frequently the camera would play them in close-up, Alyson Hannigan could probably go through an entire episode of *BTVS* in a body cast

## Performance Credits——Alyson Hannigan

**Film—*Dead Man on Campus* (1998)—Lucy**

**TV—*The Stranger Beside Me* (1995)—Dana**

**TV Credit—*Touched by an Angel* (1994)**

**TV Credit—*Almost Home* (1993)—Samantha**

**TV Credit—*Picket Fences* (1992)**

**TV—*Switched at Birth* (1991)—Gina Twigg, Age 13–16**

**TV Series Regular—*Free Spirit* (1989)—Jessie Harper**

**TV Credit—*Roseanne* (1988)—Becky's Friend #2**

**Film—*My Stepmother Is an Alien* (1988)—Jessie Mills**

**Commercial Credit—McDonald's**

**Commercial Credit—Six Flags Amusement Parks**

**Commercial Credit—Oreo Cookies**

### Best Line as Willow

**"I'm probably the only girl in school who has the coroner's office bookmarked as a favorite place!"**

**Okay, so who did her hair while she was floating around?**

and not lose her audience! It's a rare talent, one that only gets better with every stint she spends in front of the camera.

### Charisma Carpenter Charms as Cordelia Chase

A more unlikely heroine is hard to imagine than the sassy, back-talking Cordelia Chase. Once again, Whedon and crew had every opportunity to depict a stereotype, this time the typically shallow socialite who could provide a car, a nice car, but little in the way of depth or motivation. As fans swiftly came to realize, however, Charisma Carpenter and Joss Whedon had other plans for Cordelia! Though it's hard to picture now, Charisma Carpenter was originally considered for the part of Buffy! While both Sarah and Charisma are, without a doubt, strikingly talented actresses, it's hard not to consider how much we as viewers would have lost with-

## Performance Credits——Charisma Carpenter

**TV Series Regular—*Malibu Shores* (1996)—Ashley Green**

***Josh Kirby . . . Time Warrior*: "Chapter 1" (1995)—Beth Sullivan**

***Josh Kirby . . . Time Warrior*: "Chapter 2" (1995)—Beth Sullivan**

**TV Credit—*Pacific Blue* (1995)**

**TV Credit—*Baywatch* (1989)—Wendie**

**Prior to these credits, Charisma had already been featured in nearly two dozen commercials and performed as a very real cheerleader for the San Diego Chargers!**

### Best Line as Cordelia Chase

**"Darn! I have cheerleader practice tonight. Boy, I wish I knew you were gonna be digging up dead people sooner. I would've canceled."**

out each woman's individual contributions to her character. Charisma's mom may have named her after a "truly putrid" perfume by Avon, but maybe, even back on July 23, 1970, she saw something of the sparkle her daughter would bring to her roles.

## Anthony Stewart Head Turns Heads as Rupert Giles

For all the ribbing Tony Head may get because of his "elder" status among the youthful cast of *BTVS*, this forty-four-year-old draws attention from women of all ages! At last count, twenty-six Web sites were dedicated to him—the man whom one site's text describes as a "boyish British bombshell." Perhaps it's that life experience that allows him to slip so easily from the straight man

**QUESTIONS**

1. Which actress took up kickboxing after joining the *Buffy the Vampire Slayer* crew?

   A. Charisma Carpenter
   B. Alyson Hannigan
   C. Sarah Michelle Gellar
   D. Robia La Morte

2. Which *Buffy the Vampire Slayer* actor gained wild popularity for his role in a series of coffee commercials?

   A. David Boreanaz
   B. Mark Metcalf
   C. Anthony Stewart Head
   D. Nicholas Brendon

3. Which *Buffy the Vampire Slayer* regular's father is TV weatherman Dave Roberts of WPVI?

   A. Juliet Landau
   B. David Boreanaz
   C. James Marsters
   D. Seth Green

4. Which historic figure *wasn't* a prophet?

   A. An Oracle at Delphi
   B. A Vestal Virgin
   C. Ra's Priest at Memphis
   D. Apollo's Voice

## U.S. Performance Credits—Anthony Stewart Head

Commercial Credit—Taster's Choice, with Sharon Maughan (1990–1997)

TV Credit—*Jonathan Creek* (1997)—Adam Klaus

TV Series Regular—*VR.5* (1995)—Oliver Sampson

TV Credit—*Ghostbusters of East Finchley* (1995)—Terry

Film—*Royce* (1994)—Pitlock

TV Credit—*N.Y.P.D. Blue* (1993)—Nigel Gibson

TV Credit—*Highlander* (1992)

TV Credit—*The Detectives* (1989)—Simon

Film—*A Prayer for the Dying* (1987)—Rupert

TV Credit—*Boon* (1986)—Rathbone

TV Credit—*The Comic Strip Presents* (1982)—Ricki

Film—*Lady Chatterley's Lover* (1981)—Anton

TV miniseries—*Lillie* (1978)—William Le Breton

### Best Lines as Rupert Giles

Though many undoubtedly make the grade, this repartee is a list topper.

Giles: *Grave robbery? That's new, interesting.*

Buffy: *I know you meant to say gross and disturbing.*

Giles: *Yes, yes, yes, of course. Terrible thing. Must put a stop to it. Damn it.*

**Gives a whole new meaning to "necking," doesn't it?**

5. Which *Buffy the Vampire Slayer* actor will be starring in his own spin-off program in the fall of 1999?

A. David Boreanaz
B. Anthony Stewart Head
C. James Marsters
D. Nicholas Brendon

of the series's quick-paced humor to the romantically challenged stutterer to the modern-day Merlin who warns of all manner of impending doom and gloom to the easy charm of a Watcher who really can understand the vagaries of teenage love and angst—that and a working career chock-full of challenging roles!

### Robia La Morte Surprises as Jenny (a.k.a. Yanna) Calendar

Coincidence isn't a perky enough description for the happy accident that made Jenny Calendar a recurring character and gave us an opportunity to enjoy the performance of up-and-coming actress

ANSWERS

1. C

2. C

3. B

4. B

5. A

## Performance Credits—Robia La Morte

**Film**—*Spawn* (1997)—XNN Reporter

**Video Credit**—"Gett Off"—Pearl

**TV Credit**—*Beverly Hills 90210* (1990)

### Best Line as Jenny Calendar

Not surprisingly considering the incredible on-screen chemistry between Rupert and Jenny, her best line is actually a verbal duet with him.

**Rupert Giles:** *Well, I don't dangle a corkscrew from my ear!*

**Jenny Calendar:** *That's* not *where I dangle it.*

Robia La Morte. Robia La Morte didn't actually *want* to be an actress when the entertainment bug first bit. Instead, she was enjoying a successful career as a dancer when she and her partner began touring with the artist formerly known as Prince and ended

## Everything I Ever Needed to Know, I Learned from *Buffy*

† Eavesdropping doesn't work out any better in Sunnydale libraries than anywhere else.

† If you're fated to be the sacrificial virgin, you might as well dress pretty.

† Even vamps have to pay attention to the basics— like a good manicure!

† As at least one vampire discovered, riding on *top* of Cordy's car is nearly as dangerous as riding *inside* it!

# Who Was That?

EPISODE PRODUCTION NUMBER: 4V12

ORIGINAL AIR DATE: JUNE 2, 1997

WRITTEN BY: JOSS WHEDON

DIRECTED BY: JOSS WHEDON

## CAST

| | |
|---|---|
| Buffy Summers | Sarah Michelle Gellar |
| Xander Harris | Nicholas Brendon |
| Willow Rosenberg | Alyson Hannigan |
| Cordelia Chase | Charisma Carpenter |
| Rupert Giles | Anthony Stewart Head |

## GUEST CAST

| | |
|---|---|
| The Master | Mark Metcalf |
| Angel | David Boreanaz |
| Mrs. Joyce Summers | Kristine Sutherland |
| Ms. Jenny Calendar | Robia La Morte |
| The Anointed One | Andrew J. Ferchland |
| Kevin | Scott Gurney |

**Now, about that "no breath" thing . . .**

up performing in the video hit "Gett Off." Nor was her character originally intended to develop into a serious player! All things considered then, fans should feel incredibly lucky to have been granted such stellar performances in those episodes that featured the secretive Gypsy girl. Should. Though it was certainly a dramatic coup, a force that would drive the story line forward into some of its best moments, it may be some time before the fans forgive *BTVS* for depriving us of any more delightful encounters between Rupert and Jenny.

# Written on the Wall

Okay. We bite. Just how did Giles get Angel's phone number? And how did Xander know where he lived? Is he in the book, or what? And what would he be listed under?

\*   \*   \*

Oops! Who was doing Buffy's hair while she lay floating in the underground pool? Watch closely and you'll see her hair is in its sexy upsweep as the Master dumps her into the water, yet when Angel and Xander arrive, her hair is floating freely—not a stray bobby pin to be seen!

\*   \*   \*

Let's face it, there's only so much damage you can write off to your average earthquake—even in California—so, just how *did* the Slayerettes explain the skeleton in the library?

\*   \*   \*

Where *do* you hide a stake in a prom dress?

\*   \*   \*

# Season Two

**Divided they fall?**

EPISODE:

# "When She Was Bad"

N o one said dying was easy. Not even a summer vacation in sizzling L.A. with an over-indulgent father who can't say no to shoe-buying expeditions doesn't completely make up for it. No one said being best friends with a used-to-be-dead person is easy, either, and as Buffy tries to come to terms with her role, it's her nearest and dearest who bear the brunt of her anger. Somehow, it seems unlikely that the vampire community's latest attempt to resurrect the Master is going to make life better for any of Sunnydale's citizens!

the short version

## The Bad Guys

Actors know audiences just love to hate villains, that the villains always get the best lines, that they get the best death scenes, and that without a good villain, shows like *BTVS* are, if you'll excuse the pun, pointless. But finding that perfect bad guy or girl often proves trickier than anticipated. First of all, your villain has to be powerful. A wimpy villain provides no challenge for our heroes and heroines. Where's the tension in staking a guy who's cringing in a corner, or too clumsy to duck, or too stupid to create a plan with any cunning? If the Slayerettes aren't in danger, real danger, they're just another

the longer look

1. Which actress never portrayed a vampire?

   A. Sarah Michelle Gellar
   B. Bianca Lawson
   C. Kathyrn Leigh Scott
   D. Lauren Hutton

2. Which actor's film roles don't include portraying a *Buffy the Vampire Slayer* Watcher?

   A. Anthony Stewart Head
   B. Donald Sutherland
   C. Richard Riehle
   D. John Ritter

3. Which *Buffy the Vampire Slayer* actor was "discovered" while walking his dog?

   A. David Boreanaz
   B. Anthony Stewart Head
   C. Seth Green
   D. Armin Shimerman

4. Who wrote the screenplay for the *Buffy the Vampire Slayer* film?

   A. James Cameron
   B. Chris Carter
   C. Joss Whedon
   D. Christopher Wiggins

## Who Was That?

EPISODE PRODUCTION NUMBER: 5V01
ORIGINAL AIR DATE: SEPTEMBER 15, 1997
WRITTEN BY: JOSS WHEDON
DIRECTED BY: JOSS WHEDON

### CAST

| | |
|---|---|
| Buffy Summers | Sarah Michelle Gellar |
| Xander Harris | Nicholas Brendon |
| Willow Rosenberg | Alyson Hannigan |
| Cordelia Chase | Charisma Carpenter |
| Rupert Giles | Anthony Stewart Head |

### GUEST CAST

| | |
|---|---|
| Angel | David Boreanaz |
| Mrs. Joyce Summers | Kristine Sutherland |
| Hank Summers | Dean Butler |
| Ms. Jenny Calendar | Robia La Morte |
| The Anointed One | Andrew J. Ferchland |
| Tara | Tamara Braun |
| Principal Snyder | Armin Shimerman |
| Absalom | Brent Jennings |

bunch of kids with hair, skin, and hormone issues! Yet, and here's where the balance proves perilous, if our heroes are so completely outclassed that there's no hope at all, well, who wants to tune in just to see the good guys lose?

Creating an antagonist with just the right mixture of strengths, weaknesses, and prejudices is the most difficult task facing any writer. A villain needs staying power; he's got to appear week after week. The character must be capable of more than one sort of assault on our protagonist. If he's simply going to beat on her and get away each week, even cult fans' loyalty will be severely strained. If he's physically stronger, he must be emotionally or intellectually vulnerable. To fully engage the audience's emotions, to pull them into the struggle, the villain must be more than a plot device; he must have motivations, problems of his own, and above all, a goal! A long-term plan allows for the small losses and victories that all-out assaults, the huge attempts to take over the world, simply don't provide.

Not that all *BTVS*'s bad guys have been the complex tangle of evil we've just described. Some, like the Judge, fail miserably. Here was this creature, this bane of humanity, this ultimate baddie, and while he certainly had destructive potential, his part in a superhyped two-hour special was practically incidental! As Spike so clearly observed, the Judge spent most of his time sitting on his ass! In the second season's two-part finale, we're introduced to yet another beast capable of sucking the world into Hell, but once again, the stone statue does little to strike fear in the heart of anyone! For the entire first hour, it stands quietly in its box, rocking occasionally when somebody touches it, but inspiring less terror than the Pillsbury doughboy! Still, despite these apparent flaws in the accepted standard of good storytelling, they certainly serve a purpose—they highlight the real bad boys still tooling around Sunnydale! In the cases of the Judge and the beast, these apparently indestructible demons are really nothing more than tools in the hands of the master manipulators, and it's those characters, the Spikes and Drusillas, the Masters and Angels, that provide the real challenge, a challenge that satisfies even the strictest interpretation of a villain!

## Mark Metcalf Easily Mastered the Master

Working under a full-face prosthesis is sort of like living in the Buffyverse, a blessing and a curse. It can certainly establish a whole new persona, in this case quickly produce an obvious villain, and like any other mask, help an actor get into his role. It also takes away most of the techniques actors depend on to get subtle emotion

**5. Which actresses have portrayed teachers on *Buffy the Vampire Slayer*?**

A. Musetta Vander
B. Terry Cain
C. Denise Y. Dowse
D. Julie Fulton

ANSWERS

1. B

2. D

3. A

4. C

5. A, B, C, and D

## Performance Credits—Mark Metcalf

Film—*Hijacking Hollywood* (1997)—Michael Lawrence

Film—*The Stupids* (1996)—Colonel

Film—*A Reason to Believe* (1995)—Dean Kirby

Film—*Rage* (1995)—Lt. Gov. Dalquist

TV Film—*Dead Ahead: The Exxon Valdez Disaster* (1992)—Kelso

TV miniseries—*A Woman Named Jackie* (1991)—George Smathers*

TV Film—*Guilty Until Proven Innocent* (1991)—Ron D'Angelo

Film—*Oscar* (1991)—Milhous

TV Credit—*Seinfeld,* "The Doll" (1990)—Maestro

TV Credit—*Seinfeld,* "The Maestro" (1990)—Maestro

Film—*Mr. North* (1988)—Mr. Skeel

Film—*One Crazy Summer* (1986)—Aquilla Beckersted

Film—*The Heavenly Kid* (1985)—Joe

Film—*Almost You* (1984)—Andrews

Film—*The Oasis* (1984)

Film—*The Final Terror* (1981)—Mike

Film—*Where the Buffalo Roam* (1980)—Dooley

Film—*Head Over Heels* (1979)—Ox

Film—*National Lampoon's Animal House* (1978)—Doug Neidermeyer

Film—*Julia* (1977)—Pratt

* Sarah Michelle Gellar was also featured in this film as Young Jackie.

### Best Line as the Master

**"Oh, good. The feeble banter portion of the fight."**

across to their viewers. Mark Metcalf, however, despite being literally covered in prosthetics, created a villain most splendidly corrupt and subtly sinister! Having a wonderful voice didn't hurt, nor did an honest glee in his portrayal of the wonderfully wicked Master.

Unlike the purple parasite under the school, or the She-Mantis, or even the "Annoying One," the Master, despite his bizarre appearance, had entirely recognizable motives. He proved tenacious in his attempts to destroy his enemy, prepared to use force when conniving clearly wouldn't suffice. Yet, he also had vulnerabilities that arose from his individual character. It didn't really matter if he'd almost overcome his species' problem with crosses because on a very individual level, his own nature frequently betrayed him. Those specific qualities that separated him from the other vampires willing to fling themselves into a fight with the Slayer created a well-rounded character to whom audiences, on some level, could relate.

### James Marsters Gets to the Point as Spike

"Spike likes to hurt people," says James Marsters of his fiendish alter ego, and that's certainly a prerequisite for a believable villain. Spike, unlike the Anointed One, the child master he flash-fried, had an obvious agenda, one that put him in immediate and direct conflict with the town's resident Slayer. In order to restore his lady-love to health, he has to try and kill her sire—who just happens to be the Slayer's boyfriend. It's a nice, simple, even elegant scenario with which to build a relationship between the good guys and the bad guys. Spike, however, is not a simple character. Like all the best villains, he's got attitude, he's got cruelty down pat, and even at his personal worst, there's not a hint of remorse. But, he's got smarts, too: Patience and cunning are as much a part of this character as violence and rage.

For an actor, Spike is a demanding role. The moments requiring rage and near-animalistic passion usually mean acting through a prosthesis as Spike puts on his "game face," and these scenes are all-

**Best Line as Spike**

"Now, I know you haven't been in the game for a while, mate, but we still do kill people. Sort of our raison d'être, you know?"

too-frequently juxtaposed with flashes of serious sentimentality when the actor, freshly released from glue and gum, must consciously ensure he isn't still overcompensating for the now-absent prosthesis. Years of working in theater, however, have already given James Marsters that intense focus, and as his fans are discovering, his talents are translating beautifully to film and television!

### Juliet Landau Balances Drusilla

Goals, motivation, and the capacity for cruelty are certainly intrinsic to a good villain, but, as with heroes, the potential to grow adds a new edginess to roles that can be easily typecast. Both Marsters and Landau have proven conclusively that they and their characters remain incredibly adaptive. For Spike, a less-than-stellar outing against the Slayer left our bad-boy punk-vamp to deal with a severe physical impediment to his schemes. The character of Drusilla has, in ironic reflection, gone from simpering, slightly psychotic invalid to simpering, slightly psychotic powerhouse! Where Spike's disability has brought forth the character's craftiness, Dru's sudden recovery added a completely different, highly physical aspect to the role. These opposing sides provide a multitude of new possibilities for interaction, drastically extending the longevity of these characters.

Of course, it also puts new demands on the actors portraying these characters and, in a few short months, Juliet Landau has carried off every personality change, every twisted emotion with the élan and professional competence you'd expect from someone born into the family of working actors. As the daughter of Martin Landau and Barbara Bain, she's seen years of dedication pay off, and if her own filmography is any indication, is more than willing to pay her dues in ever more contradictory roles.

## Performance Credits——Juliet Landau

**Film—*Ravager* (1997)—Sarra**

**Film—*Life Among the Cannibals* (1996)**

**Film—*Theodore Rex* (1995)—Dr. Shade**

**Film—*Ed Wood* (1994)—Loretta King**

**Film—*Direct Hit* (1994)—Shelly**

**Film—*Neon City* (1992)—Twink**

**Film—*Pump Up the Volume* (1990)—Teri**

**Film—*The Grifters* (1990)—Young Lilly**

**TV Credit—*Parker Lewis Can't Lose* (1990)—Lucinda**

### Best Line as Drusilla

**"I've named them [the stars] all the same name and there's terrible confusion."**

## Almost an Angel, David Boreanaz

The Master, for all his great ghoulishness, never really changed. Juliet Landau had several episodes in which to exhibit her character's growing strength and confidence. James Marsters had more of a wrench with Spike's sudden reduction in mobility, but everyone took it for granted that, like Drusilla, he'd soon be back to full strength, a return to the status quo, but better because of Dru's equal status. David Boreanaz faced a completely different challenge when a Gypsy curse turned the previously principled Angel into Angelus, a demon-ridden monster without the checks and balances once provided by Angel's evicted soul. The two characters couldn't have been more different if he'd been hired to portray Mr. Rogers and the Terminator!

For a young actor, the switch is a valuable exercise. For fans of *Buffy the Vampire Slayer*, it provides drama and conflict on a com-

99

## Performance Credits——David Boreanaz

**TV Credit—*Married . . . with Children***

**Film—*Aspen Extreme* (1993)—uncredited**

**Film—*Best of the Best II* (1993)—uncredited**

### Best Line as Angel

**"You've got a lot to learn about men, kiddo, although I guess you proved that last night."**

pletely different scale. Physical dangers can be controlled, prepared for, anticipated. Against the emotional ambush audiences walked into as they watched Angel become Angelus, there was no defense. An old storytelling axiom advises writers to force their hero up a tree, and once he's almost to the last branch that could possibly support him, throw rocks at him! In Angelus, Whedon and company have created a villain with not only the strength, purpose, and determination to destroy his heroine, but a villain in whom his heroine has a deeply personal stake. Angelus could kill Buffy a

## Everything I Ever Needed to Know, I Learned from *Buffy*

† Having a vampire for a boyfriend should give new meaning to the phrase "in-laws from Hell."

† Killing, wantonly and passionately, is a fine way to distract vampires.

† It's easier to work out your issues with a sledgehammer in your hand.

† Asking a librarian how he spent his summer is, well, redundant if you know how he spends the other three seasons.

## Written on the Wall

Continuity within a series is a wonderful thing. It makes audiences go "Oooh, isn't that so-and-so?" and step a smidgen closer to that much sought-after state called "suspension of disbelief." Fans love seeing familiar faces float through the background of scenes, but in this episode, at least one reappearance was more unsettling than satisfying. See the kid in the purply shirt, wandering by the school fountain? It's Owen from "Never Kill a Boy on the First Date"! Unfortunately, it's *precisely* the same footage. No one expects every frame of every episode to be new or unique, but using stock footage with recognizable guest stars re-enacting their prior appearances is definitely disturbing.

\* \* \*

And speaking of continuity . . . You don't have to be watching too closely to notice Buffy's shirt change from shell-pink during her scenes in Mom's car to white in the subsequent school scenes and back to pink before nightfall! Even Buffy isn't such a clotheshorse that she'd strip off her clothes on her way across the lawn!

\* \* \*

thousand times before he ever laid a hand on her. With their former intimacy turned into a weapon, Angelus is the ultimate antagonist. Next to him, a demon capable of sucking in the entire world looks more like a ridiculous garden gnome.

No healthy, red-blooded, prepubescent (or pubescent, for that matter!) man would consider any of Cordelia's parts disposable!

# EPISODE:
## "Some Assembly Required"

the short version

A s if a Slayer living on top of a Hellmouth didn't have enough vampires and demons to keep an eye on! Now, something else, something new, something human, is digging up Sunnydale's already-busy graveyards—something with a liking for the body parts of young cheerleaders. Dead women tell no tales, but it's the living ones Buffy has to worry about when their body snatcher goes after warmer prey.

## There's Gold in Them There Graves!

the longer look

*If not for scientists, there'd be no grave robbing!*
*—William Burke, 1829, on the occasion of his hanging*
*for the crime of body snatching*

Burke was certainly in a position to know. Burke, and his partner in crime, Hare, who helped run a dilapidated boardinghouse in an even more dilapidated section of Edinburgh, both quickly discovered that selling stiffs to Dr. Knox's Anatomy School was infinitely more profitable than feeding and housing the vagrants in their live forms. It all started innocently enough, when a tenant already well behind in his rent died in his room without a coin in his pocket. Hearing that a local doctor was looking for bodies to use in his dissection

103

## Who Was That?

**EPISODE PRODUCTION NUMBER: 5V02**

**ORIGINAL AIR DATE: SEPTEMBER 22, 1997**

**WRITTEN BY: TY KING**

**DIRECTED BY: BRUCE SETH GREEN**

### CAST

| | |
|---|---|
| **Buffy Summers** | **Sarah Michelle Gellar** |
| **Xander Harris** | **Nicholas Brendon** |
| **Willow Rosenberg** | **Alyson Hannigan** |
| **Cordelia Chase** | **Charisma Carpenter** |
| **Rupert Giles** | **Anthony Stewart Head** |

### GUEST CAST

| | |
|---|---|
| **Angel** | **David Boreanaz** |
| **Ms. Jenny Calendar** | **Robia La Morte** |
| **Eric** | **Michael Bacall** |
| **Chris** | **Angelo Spizzirri** |
| **Daryl** | **Ingo Neuhaus** |
| **Mrs. Epps** | **Melanie MacQueen** |
| **Cheerleader** | **Amanda Wilmshurst** |

classes, they decided to sell the body to pay the debt. While the man's family might have objected—had anyone bothered to contact them *before* selling him off—Hare and Burke had done absolutely nothing illegal at that point. Irksome and immoral by the standards of the day, certainly, but legal, since a dead body, then as now, had absolutely no rights for anyone to violate.

As with Chris and Eric, Sunnydale's grave-robbing duo, it was the *live* bodies that landed Burke and Hare in trouble. Fifteen corpses later, the startling mortality rate at Hare's Boarding House was becoming common knowledge and the "freshness and warmth" of their cadavers aroused considerable comment from students used to dealing with much more pungent bodies. When the attractive body of Mary Docherty, one of Edinburgh's most popular prostitutes, crossed the table—and was instantly recognized by many of the students—Burke and Hare's lucrative little enterprise stalled completely. Dozens of witnesses could testify to the excellent condition of the woman's body just hours before she turned up dead and, with cries of murder already flying about, it didn't take Hare long to decide that he'd be better off selling out his partner than taking his chances in front of the jury. Hare was run out of town. Burke was hanged, and like many of the other corpses resulting from legal executions, was soon lying on the cold marble of an anatomist's table and his public dissection was attended by hundreds!

Knox, who purchased fourteen suspiciously fresh corpses, was never charged with anything.

## Everything I Ever Needed to Know, I Learned from *Buffy*

† Two hundred and forty-one years old can still be cool.

† Open graves and high heels don't mix.

† Paying for food, especially Mexican, can definitely lead to a "thing."

† Having the coroner's office among your Web-page bookmarks doesn't help your dating reputation.

† Talking to an empty chair is a sure sign of impending wackydom.

† Field trips shouldn't include the local graveyard.

† When librarians and vampires get more action than a seventeen-year-old with healthy hormones, it's time to try a new pickup line!

**QUESTIONS**

1. **Which actors have portrayed Frankenstein's
   monster?**

   A. **Robert De Niro**
   B. **Boris Karloff**
   C. **Nick Brimble**
   D. **Michael Sarrazin**

2. **Which actress was cast
   as the lead in *Bride of
   Frankenstein*?**

   A. **Elsa Lanchester**
   B. **Catherine Deneuve**
   C. **Lauren Hutton**
   D. **Audrey Hepburn**

3. **Who plays the ultimate
   bloodsucker in the film
   *Buffy the Vampire Slayer*?**

   A. **Mark Metcalf**
   B. **David Boreanaz**
   C. **Tom Cruise**
   D. **Rutger Hauer**

4. **Who penned the original
   *Frankenstein* novel?**

   A. **Bram Stoker**
   B. **Lord Byron**
   C. **Mary Wollstonecraft
      Shelley**
   D. **Jules Verne**

5. **Which fictional creature
   has no folkloric tradition?**

   A. **Dracula**
   B. **Werewolf**
   C. **Frankenstein's monster**
   D. **Incubus**

**The Frankenstein character captured film audiences as easily as
book lovers when portrayed by the likes of Boris Karloff, 1931.**

In a decidedly morbid, not to mention gross, way, Chris and Eric were actually following in the footsteps of some great men. Michelangelo, Leonardo da Vinci, and Raphael turned to body snatching for the sake of their art. Hippocrates, whose Oath is still part of the medical profession today, encouraged his students to snatch bodies whenever possible in order to increase their anatomical knowledge. Sir Isaac Newton, Charles Darwin, and Francis Bacon all tacitly agreed with the practice of paying professional grave robbers to procure the bodies necessary to fulfill the needs of doctors and scientists. As Dr. Ahbram Schiell noted, "Without some sacrifice on the part of the masses, the progress of humanity stops here."

The "masses," however, who were providing, willingly or not, nearly 95 percent of the "sacrifice," couldn't help noting that the schools got their bodies, the grave robbers got their coins, and the families of the deceased got absolutely nothing!

At the height of the body-snatching era, whole new professions sprang up in response to graveyard predations. Coffins, which even for the well-to-do had never been particularly substantial affairs, progressed from pine boxes to lead-lined marble creations sealed with iron bolts. Botcher and Crewe offered a "Theft-proof Receptacle" nearly ten feet square that more resembled a Chinese-box puzzle than a traditional coffin. Sliding panels allowed the deceased to be tucked into one of eight possible positions and were thought to deter a grave robber by making him hunt about for the corpse. The box even came with a little sign designed to be stuck in the ground for the first few weeks, sort of an early version of the *These Premises Protected by* stickers handed out by modern-day security companies. For about half of what a body snatcher could get for dear Aunt Titania's corpse, the grieving family could hire a grave-sitter who literally sat atop a new grave and beat off all com-

## Written on the Wall

This episode marks the first overhaul of *Buffy*'s introduction and opening credits. No longer does an unknown narrator drone out the whole Buffy myth. Instead, Anthony Stewart Head, who plays Buffy's Watcher, tells the tale, adding a rich—and pertinent—voice to the throbbing music and vivid imagery. Finally! A total package.

\* \* \*

Just how many pictures did Eric take of his intended victim? None of the ones we see in his homemade jigsaw puzzle came from the impromptu photo session he staged in the hallway.

\* \* \*

Ummm? Just why did the shovel disappear?

\* \* \*

**ANSWERS**

**1. A, B, C, and D**

**2. A**

**3. D**

**4. C**

**5. C**

ers until the corpse, following the normal course of decay, became less appealing to the members of the College of Barbers and Surgeons. Of course, that solution depended on the grave-sitter not being on the payroll of any of the highly organized grave robbers!

Mary Shelley's *Frankenstein*, written during a resurgence of the body-snatching craze, not only illustrated the current fear of science spiraling ahead of ethical understanding, but the Victorian's horror of postmortem examinations. Remember, in Shelley's tale, Dr. Frankenstein was the real monster and his crime, in addition to aspiring to Godlike powers, was creating a piecemeal body from scavenged corpses. Shelley and her audience would have been well aware that not all bodies sent to the tables were actually dead!

Numerous well-publicized incidents of bodies reanimating after death were already making the rounds of Victorian society when the body-snatching phenomenon became headline news, so it was only a matter of time before reanimated corpses found their way into the classroom. One such case appears in *The Newgate Calendar*. A German surgeon, about to begin his postmortem exam on one of the criminals' bodies that came to his facility from the gallows, turned to his students, and with his hand resting on the "dead" man's chest, said, "I am pretty certain, gentlemen, from the warmth of the subject and the flexibility of the limbs, that by a proper degree of attention and care the vital heat would return, and life in consequence take place. But, when it is considered what a rascal we should again have among us, that he was hanged for so cruel a murder, and that, should we restore him to life, he would probably kill somebody else, I say, gentlemen, all these things considered, it is my opinion that we had better proceed with the dissection." And he did, despite what one student described as "numerous twitchings which greatly impeded the view."

Small wonder that "scientists" were viewed as amoral, sadistic creatures!

Small wonder that the "masses" fully believed them capable of bringing a jigsaw body to life.

Small wonder the story should horrify and titillate even a modern audience so that, like the readers of Shelley's time, *Buffy* fans should still find the tale so engrossing.

# "School Hard"

This is going to be a busy weekend for Buffy. The vampires want her for dinner at the Feast of St. Vigeous. Principal Snyder and her mother want her for Parent-Teacher Night. Giles wants her to practice, practice, practice. Sheila wants to dump her—or on her. And, to top it all off, her sort-of-boyfriend's family is coming to visit! How's a Slayer to juggle all that?

the short version

## Daddy, Dearest

When *Dracula* hit Victorian bookshelves, the typical vampire was a lone wolf, a mysterious stranger with an interest in Victorian ladies. He was sexy, scary, and *single*. He might keep a harem of vampiric "wives," but they were mere conveniences. The Count most certainly *wasn't* a family man. His victims, even his wives, slaved on his behalf. They didn't give him any backtalk, they didn't question his leadership, and they certainly didn't hoist him up into a shaft of sunlight!

Modern audiences, however, want their heroes and heroines revealed layer by layer, gradually disclosing all their strengths and foibles for close examination—and they want to know the who and why of the villains presented as fair matches for those heroes. In the intervening hundred years, authors and film-

the longer look

1. Who hasn't portrayed a television vampire?

    A. Brian Thompson
    B. James Marsters
    C. Juliet Landau
    D. Alyson Hannigan

2. Who does the dog named Bertha Blue belong to?

    A. Alyson Hannigan
    B. Charisma Carpenter
    C. James Marsters
    D. David Boreanaz

3. Who says of his character, "He's a psychopath, but I'm good with that"?

    A. David Boreanaz
    B. Seth Green
    C. James Marsters
    D. Robin Sachs

4. Which actress's father played a theatrical Dracula in 1984?

    A. Sarah Michelle Gellar
    B. Juliet Landau
    C. Julie Benz
    D. Musetta Vander

5. Who ran his own theatrical company?

    A. Seth Green
    B. James Marsters
    C. David Boreanaz
    D. Ken Lerner

**What a face! He must have tasted Buffy's lemonade!**

makers have found it useful to satisfy those desires, and vampires have developed their own supporting cast of characters in the form of vampiric "families." "Sires," "clans," and "coteries" now supply the secondary cast of cohorts for the antiheroes of vampire fiction, including Anne Rice's *Interview with the Vampire* and its related works, television programs like *Kindred: The Embraced*, and, of course, *Buffy the Vampire Slayer.*

Trying to keep track of those affiliations ain't easy. Try this on. The Master made Darla, who made Angel, so he's Angel's grandsire. Right. Angel made Spike, so Angel is Spike's sire. Okay. Now, in the meantime, the Master made the Anointed One and became

110

# Who Was That?

**EPISODE PRODUCTION NUMBER: 5V03**

**ORIGINAL AIR DATE: SEPTEMBER 29, 1997**

**STORY WRITTEN BY: JOSS WHEDON AND DAVID GREENWALT**

**TELEPLAY WRITTEN BY: DAVID GREENWALT**

**DIRECTED BY: JOHN T. KRETCHMER**

---

## CAST

| | |
|---|---|
| Buffy Summers | Sarah Michelle Gellar |
| Xander Harris | Nicholas Brendon |
| Willow Rosenberg | Alyson Hannigan |
| Cordelia Chase | Charisma Carpenter |
| Rupert Giles | Anthony Stewart Head |

## GUEST CAST

| | |
|---|---|
| Mrs. Joyce Summers | Kristine Sutherland |
| Angel | David Boreanaz |
| Ms. Jenny Calendar | Robia La Morte |
| The Anointed One | Andrew J. Ferchland |
| Spike | James Marsters |
| Drusilla | Juliet Landau |
| Sheila | Alexandra Johnes |
| Principal Snyder | Armin Shimerman |
| Brian Kirch | Alan Abelew |
| Parent | Keith MacKechnie |
| Helpless Girl | Joanie Pleasant |

ANSWERS

1. D

2. D

3. C

4. B

5. B

## Everything I Ever Needed to Know, I Learned from *Buffy*

✝ The '60s were a psychedelically challenged
   era for vampiredom.

✝ Stake whittling is a Saturday night kinda thing—
   in Sunnydale.

✝ *"Le vache doit me touche de la jeudi"* makes sense—
   in Sunnydale.

✝ The Hellmouth—the best in vampiric resort spas.

✝ The three prerequisites for vampire slaying? Stakes,
   a mother with an ax, and foundation.

✝ Being killed only gets you dead; being expelled
   gets you grounded!

✝ Never let an ax-wielding vampire guard your back.

✝ "Gang-related PCP" covers a multitude of sins.

✝ Saving your mother's life should at least get you *un*grounded.

*his* sire. So, what does that make Spike and the Anointed One? In a normal family, the Anointed One would be Spike's much younger great-uncle! And, seeing as Spike and Drusilla were both made by Angel, then this devoted couple would, in a normal family, be considered brother and sister as well as lovers. (Which, incidentally, makes the Master their great-grandfather.) Almost makes Angel's interest in Drusilla seem ordinary, doesn't it?

Vampires and taboos remain as inseparable now as they were during the Victorian era; it's just our taboos that have changed. In 1897, any discussion of sex brought down the wrath of society. The subject of discussion didn't have to be an incestuous or multiple relationship; it simply had to be about anything sexual. Nice young Victorian ladies were, it seems, more easily titillated than the women of 1997. Any tall, dark, handsome guy, though preferably one with a nice Old World title, who regularly invaded women's boudoirs at night, to steal their blood or their virginity, already smacked of the illicit, the forbidden.

When *Dracula* was released, marriage was as much an institution as a rite. Marriage gave a woman prestige, a place in the social circle, and—should she survive her husband and manage to inherit his estate—freedom. A married woman, in the company of other suitably married women, could walk along the boardwalk without an elderly relative to chaperon her. She could order her own meals, and order about whatever staff her husband chose to provide. She could shop on her own—from the careful allotment of monies her husband chose to give her, even if the money brought into the marriage was hers. In return for all these privileges, only three things were asked of her: One, never think about sex; two, never form any opinions about sex; and three, never discuss sex. In this highly repressive society, the vampire quickly became a romanticized antihero who thumbed his nose at the social regime. A vampire novel, while draped in the trappings of the horrific, was the Victorian era's version of a sizzling romance!

Since then, real sizzlers have hit the shelves, and in retrospect, the Victorian vampire has become something almost pathetic, a man of extraordinary powers who can't get a date without slipping her the Mickey first! If it wasn't for those horrific elements, which were little more than window dressing in 1897, a 1990s kind of woman would laugh Stoker's Dracula right back to his box!

To push vampires out to the edge of society once again, new limits must be found, new taboos broken and, well, as they say, the more things change, the more they stay the same, so the taboos today's vampires are breaking are—surprise!—sexual, but different.

The muddled relationships of modern vampires, the intricate family trees that can make the same person your sister, your aunt, and your mother simultaneously, allow new wordsmiths to dabble in even murkier waters. What's a little incest between family, right? And, when your "mother" is also your "sire," gender becomes almost passé. Even killing takes on a new scope when simple homicide turns into fratricide, patricide, and, in a strange sense, regicide.

**You'd think a couple with such quantities of cool would have more than three outfits, wouldn't you? One red dress, one white dress, and one black dress do not a wardrobe make, really.**

What vampire fiction has always done, what it continues to do, is overturn the accepted norm. It's what gives Spike and Dru's bizarre little romance its spice. It's what startles us when the old order (or is that the young order in case of the Anointed One?) is overthrown. It's what intrigues us when a Slayer falls in love with a vampire. Always a commentary on its times, *Buffy the Vampire Slayer* is following in some heavyweight traditions—and entertaining us in the bargain!

Some things never change, like the fact that *every* episode of *Buffy the Vampire Slayer* must include at least one continuity blooper! Watch the books that Buffy and Willow leave on their table at The Bronze. One dance later, they come back, and their homework really has been stolen! Think Jenny Calendar is gonna believe Bronzers are that desperate for assignments?

And, what about the mysteriously mobile trophy case? When Cordelia and Willow take their dive into the utility closet to escape the vampire invasion, it's right next to the door. Just two scenes later, it's on the opposite side of the corridor! Oh, and, by the way, why would the school put emergency power lights *in* the trophy case, but not in the halls themselves?

Just to prove the pervasiveness of the blooper epidemic, they even combined a blooper from last season with this season's new menace. If, as Angel claimed while standing over Buffy's soaking body in "Prophecy Girl," he has no breath, what exactly is Spike doing with that cigarette? He certainly seems to have no problem inhaling!

\* \* \*

Okay. It's definite. Nothing short of SPF 2000 sunblock will save a Buffyverse vampire from dying in sunlight. Oddly enough, though vamp mythology has been common throughout the world's cultures, it wasn't until Bram Stoker's *Dracula* that the notion of sunlight's danger to vamps was introduced; few mythologies even postulated that daylight and vampires didn't mix. Since then, it's become a de rigueur feature of the breed.

\* \* \*

**Ampata was right—Buffy is no "ordinary girl."**

# " Inca Mummy Girl "

T hings are getting interesting at Sunnydale. Not only are Buffy and the gang being hauled off to look at the remains of a society that's been dead for hundreds of years—like Buffy didn't have enough dealings with dead things?—but they're about to be inundated with *exchange students*. Yet more people for Buffy to hide her secret identity from! Could things get any better? Only if your definition of *better* includes a life-sucking mummy, the latest monster attracted to this one-Starbuck Hellmouth.

the short version

## You Say Ampata, I Say Ampato

If the name of Buffy's latest problem child left you with a vague sense of déjà vu, or a right-on-the-tip-of-your-tongue feeling, you'll probably remember, with a little nudging, the story of the real Ampato Maiden. In fact, even if you're not into archaeology, don't have a clue who the Incas were, and didn't know PBS was a television network, you'd have been hard-pressed not to have seen some mention of this anthropological miracle sometime during the summer of 1997.

Like the Buffyverse's "Ampata," the Ampato Maiden was a teenage Peruvian girl, probably from a small village somewhere

the longer look

117

# Who Was That?

**EPISODE PRODUCTION NUMBER:** 5V04

**ORIGINAL AIR DATE:** OCTOBER 6, 1997

**WRITTEN BY:** MATT KIENE AND JOE REINKEMEYER

**DIRECTED BY:** ELLEN PRESSMAN

---

## CAST

| | |
|---|---|
| Buffy Summers | Sarah Michelle Gellar |
| Xander Harris | Nicholas Brendon |
| Willow Rosenberg | Alyson Hannigan |
| Cordelia Chase | Charisma Carpenter |
| Rupert Giles | Anthony Stewart Head |

## GUEST CAST

| | |
|---|---|
| Mrs. Joyce Summers | Kristine Sutherland |
| Oz | Seth Green |
| Ampata/Mummy | Ara Celi |
| Peruvian Boy/Ampata | Samuel Jacobs |
| Gwen | Kristen Winnicki |
| Devon | Jason Hall |
| Peru Man | Gil Birmingham |
| Sven | Henrik Rosvall |
| Rodney | Joey Crawford |
| Jonathan | Danny Strong |

high in the Andes just over five hundred years ago and, like Ampata, she got to know more about mummies than anyone would want to.

The real Ampato Maiden, a tiny girl with shiny black hair, brilliant white teeth, dark eyes, and, if computerized CT scans are to be believed, one of the deepest sets of dimples ever, might never have been found at all if not for a volcanic eruption above the 20,700-foot mark near the snow-covered summit of Mount Ampato—circumstances too dramatic for even *BTVS* to reproduce. The archaeologist credited with the Maiden's discovery, Dr. Johan Reinhard, had, in fact, already surveyed and dismissed the Ampato site as unworthy of further archaeological study! Even after the eruption, the Maiden might well have remained hidden for hundreds of years longer if exotically colored bird feathers, some from a flamingo headdress she was still wearing, hadn't been washed downhill with her during the melt caused by hot ashes landing on the mountain's icy slope.

As an anthropologic find, the Ampato Maiden is truly unique. Buried in icy ground, well above the snowline, her body froze completely within hours of her death. Not only were her garments (including finely woven alpaca fabrics and elaborately detailed linens) like new when she was found, her body never had a chance to decay! Unlike most mummies, which are dried and brittle, the Ampato Maiden's skin was soft and smooth. Said one observer, "Her face and neck are wrinkled, but her arms and torso, even her legs and feet, are so finely preserved that you can see a tiny freckle on one foot, the tan lines on her arms!" The internal preservation floored everyone. Internal organs, the most delicate portions of any preserved specimen, have never been found in a naturally mummi-

## Everything I Ever Needed to Know, I Learned from *Buffy*

† Even mummies have fashion issues.

† Teen dances are the natural environment
for undercover Slayers.

† Any relationship that doesn't include a praying
mantis or a mummy has potential!

### QUESTIONS

1. **Who played the mummy in the original *The Mummy*?**

   A. Boris Karloff

   B. Lon Chaney, Sr.

   C. Lon Chaney, Jr.

   D. Bela Lugosi

2. **Who was born November 5, 1949?**

   A. Anthony Stewart Head

   B. Robia La Morte

   C. James Marsters

   D. Armin Shimerman

3. **Which of these movies never existed?**

   A. *Abbott and Costello Meet the Invisible Man*

   B. *Abbott and Costello Meet the Mummy*

   C. *Abbott and Costello Meet Frankenstein*

   D. *Abbott and Costello Meet Dracula*

4. **In which country would an Incan mummy most likely be found?**

   A. Canada

   B. Russia

   C. Peru

   D. Haiti

5. **In what year was the original *The Mummy* released?**

   A. 1919

   B. 1925

   C. 1932

   D. 1956

fied specimen. Even the Egyptian mummies, which were buried with crematory vessels to hold a number of organs, couldn't compare to a completely chemical-free preservation like this! Considering the quality of the site specimens (two other figures were also found, though not so well preserved), it's hardly surprising that the Ampato Maiden stirred such interest in academic circles. What *was* surprising was the intense *public* response generated as she and her auxiliary displays toured the United States.

"There's something so . . . vulnerable about her," says Maisie McCarthy, a fourteen-year-old who saw the exhibit in New York. "She's just sitting there, so . . . so real! And, thinking that she died *by choice*! That blows me away!"

In that respect, the Ampato Maiden and Ampata differ dramatically. Where Ampata seemed willing to destroy almost anyone to maintain herself, the Ampato Maiden probably *did* submit willingly, even happily, to her sacrifice. With so relatively "fresh" a specimen, archaeologists were able to perform testing impossible to do on desiccated figures. Despite the ease with which this body could be examined, no piece of evidence indicates the Ampato Maiden was abused or even struggled with her killers. Not a single mark mars that perfect skin, not a bruise, not a scratch, not so much as a typical teenage blemish!

What they did find was a well-muscled, well-fed, healthy young woman with a single skull fracture just above one eye and a brain that had shifted markedly from that break. Sidney Copely, professor of forensic medicine, believes this tells us a lot about the Ampato Maiden, her people, and her culture. "There's no real doubt that she died of a single blow to the head—and that it *wasn't* accidental. They certainly intended her to die, but if you consider the options available to them, the rather horrific practices we *know* they used against their enemies, well, there's no comparison. It wasn't euthanasia, but there's no doubt they never intended for her to suffer, this was the *easiest* way they could accomplish their aim. There are other indications, too. From a small spot of vomit on her clothes, we can be reasonably certain she was, one, either drugged with one of a number of local plants; two, drunk on the corn beer;

**Even a "one-Starbucks town" is more lively than this!**

or three, both. It's more likely than not that she never felt the blow that killed her. And the blow wasn't random, either. If you can associate the words 'surgical precision' with a pre-Columbian society, well, that's what this was." He chuckles. "I imagine that, somewhere, there was a 'specialist' involved who probably took home a fee equal to our better surgeons'." The laughter fades. "The Ampato Maiden died quietly, quickly, with virtually no pain. That's more than we can offer a lot of people today."

If you do happen to have more than a passing interest in the discovery of near-perfectly preserved girls on Peruvian hillsides, you may well have gotten a chuckle out of Ampata's arrival in Sunnydale by bus. When Reinhard transported Mount Ampato's unique specimen—the artifact that would later receive *armed* escort from the university that housed her to the National Geographic Society offices; the teenager who would command complete attention from some of the world's most celebrated minds—he had to carry his discovery by mule and bus for nearly fourteen hours!

ANSWERS

1. A

2. D

3. D

4. C

5. D

# Written on the Wall

Oops! Even corpses have a nightlife in Sunnydale. See how the mummy in Ampata's trunk shifts sides in between Buffy's first and second attempts to lift the lid on the trunk?

\* \* \*

Buffy is a worse student than a guy who thinks there are just "fourteen natural elements"? Hey, Buffy, it really *is* time for you to get a tutor!

\* \* \*

If you've seen the film *A Cry in the Dark,* based on the real-life story of Lindy Chamberlain, who claimed that wild dogs stole her child while she was camping in the Australian outback, you've already got the inspiration for the band name Dingoes Ate My Baby. There is no such real band; the sounds you hear are from none other than Four Star Mary, a band worth checking out.

\* \* \*

Continuity blooper! Well, you knew there had to be at least one per episode, right? Watch Xander's gym bag during his tussle with the bodyguard. Despite a clear view of it tumbling down several sections of bleacher seats, it's right back in its original place when Xander finally grabs it up and runs.

\* \* \*

Cordelia drives. Oz drives. *Xander* drives! No wonder Buffy *needs* that driver's license! Imagine entrusting yourself to a guy who was nearly sucked into mummydom! It's about time they updated the prerequisites for Slayers to include "valid driver's license and own transportation."

\* \* \*

# "Reptile Boy"

**B**uffy's "sacred duty" is beginning to nip too tightly, and her "relationship" with Angel is going absolutely nowhere, when Cordy dangles before her the opportunity to attend a college frat party with a handsome, warm-bodied young man. Party? Patrol? Party? Patrol? No contest! After arranging a cover story to fool both her mother and her Watcher, Buffy's off to get down with the Delta Zeta Kappas. The party, however, fails to live up to its billing, and it doesn't take long for Buffy to realize that these strangers are a lot stranger than she'd imagined!

the short version

## Hazing: The Real Ritual

The real appeal of shows such as *Buffy the Vampire Slayer* is their ability to simultaneously engage an audience on so many levels. Watching *Buffy* borders on a bizarre form of voyeurism, as though through these characters, we peek at ourselves. It doesn't matter that half the audience can identify with *Giles* as easily as Buffy, that viewers might have been in high school thirty or just three years ago, because *BTVS* spans that generation gap, focusing on experiences so universal that its audience's age is immaterial. Sure, the bands, the clothes, and yeah, the hair, have changed, but the bedrock this program is built on,

the longer look

123

## QUESTIONS

1. Which *Buffy the Vampire Slayer* regular has a golden retriever named Sydney?

   A. David Boreanaz
   B. Charisma Carpenter
   C. Sarah Michelle Gellar
   D. Anthony Stewart Head

2. Which of the following actors appeared in drag on *Buffy the Vampire Slayer*?

   A. Sarah Michelle Gellar
   B. Alyson Hannigan
   C. Charisma Carpenter
   D. Nicholas Brendon

3. What do Suzan Bagdadi, Jeri Baker, Dugg Kirkpatrick, Susan Carol Schwary, and Francine Shermaine have in common?

   A. They've all been staked on *Buffy the Vampire Slayer.*
   B. They've all been bitten on *Buffy the Vampire Slayer.*
   C. They've all been vampires on *Buffy the Vampire Slayer.*
   D. They were all nominated for an Emmy in the category "Outstanding Hairstyling for a Series" while working on *Buffy the Vampire Slayer.*

**Think they blew the whole season's prosthetics budget on this one?**

the *emotional* landscape, is timeless. Take away the vampires and stakes and you're left with a show about people engaged in some very recognizable situations.

"Reptile Boy," despite its demon-in-the-basement script, drags viewers in because its situations remain so intrinsically *human*.

The trick with any character-driven, message-heavy episode is to make us care about the characters and to coat the message until it becomes somewhat digestible. Xander in a wig and stiletto heels, wearing a size 40DDD bra, is eminently digestible, making the very real existence of fraternity hazing part of the story line without hammering home the dangers in a documentary-style yawnfest.

Only afterward does the comic image play on the viewer's imag-

124

ination and bring other, less laughable, incidents to mind. Incidents like the senseless death in 1994 of Mike Davis, a student at Southeast Missouri State University, whose "Hell Week" activities included being a punching bag for his soon-to-be fraternity brothers—and his was only one of *twenty-four* murders, which, between 1983 and 1996, have been incontrovertibly linked to hazing.

Luckily, not all hazing rituals lead to death. Since 1987, many states have adopted laws defining and proscribing hazing acts and

---

## Who Was That?

**EPISODE PRODUCTION NUMBER: 5V05**

**ORIGINAL AIR DATE: OCTOBER 13, 1997**

**WRITTEN BY: DAVID GREENWALT**

**DIRECTED BY: DAVID GREENWALT**

---

### CAST

| | |
|---|---|
| Buffy Summers | Sarah Michelle Gellar |
| Xander Harris | Nicholas Brendon |
| Willow Rosenberg | Alyson Hannigan |
| Cordelia Chase | Charisma Carpenter |
| Rupert Giles | Anthony Stewart Head |

### GUEST CAST

| | |
|---|---|
| Angel | David Boreanaz |
| Tom | Todd Babcock |
| Richard | Greg Vaughn* |
| Callie | Jordana Spiro |

* Though spelled *Vaughn* during the on-screen credits, it's actually *Vaughan*.

---

4. **Which of these classic SF films *didn't* feature some poor schmuck who had to squirm into the rubber suit every day?**

   A. *Creature from the Black Lagoon*
   B. *E.T.—The Extra-Terrestrial*
   C. *Howard the Duck*
   D. *Swamp Thing*

5. **Which *Buffy the Vampire Slayer* regular's mother portrayed Mrs. Magret in the Magret mysteries for BBC?**

   A. James Marsters
   B. Armin Shimerman
   C. Anthony Stewart Head
   D. David Boreanaz

ANSWERS

1. B

2. D

3. D

4. B

5. C

## Everything I Ever Needed to Know, I Learned from *Buffy*

† Nothing good lives in the basement.

† "Surround-sound" dreams are a sure sign of impending crushdom.

† "Slipping into something more comfortable" shouldn't include monk robes!

† Leaving a party in a bra you didn't bring with you just isn't a good thing.

have rigorously enforced laws designed to curb them. At least three different levels of hazing are currently recognized, with the definitions and repercussions for such acts being better developed each year.

Low-level hazing can include:

- **Requiring pledges to use separate entrances, hygiene facilities, or eating areas (One pledge was required to eat a meal served atop a toilet.)**

- **Requiring pledges to perform personal servitude that is demeaning (A University of Texas pledge was forced to sweep a path around campus for a senior.)**

- **Requiring pledges to perform constant, useless activities within the frat house**

- **Requiring a pledge to adopt degrading, embarrassing, or ridiculous dress (There's one Xander could identify with!)**

- **Requiring minor legal infractions (i.e., keying cars, petty theft, etc.) of pledges**

- **Requiring a pledge to respond vocally to particular phrases or circumstances**

Recognized midlevel hazing rituals include:

- **Requiring pledges to go without sleep for more than twenty-four hours**

- Requiring a pledge to be totally—or partially in some states—undressed (Again, Xander can relate!)

- Requiring a pledge to ignore personal hygiene through intimidation, or deprivation of hygiene facilities

- Requiring a pledge to submit to "body painting," the practice of covering a pledge with a foreign substance, which might include, but not be restricted to, tar and feathers, syrups, oils, other food substances, body fluids or wastes, and any physically harmful substances

- Requiring pledges to undergo verbal abuse/humiliation/interrogation

High-level hazing rituals are normally seen as those that possibly or will cause physical harm or death. While some frat chapters have proven quite imaginative in dreaming up abuses to heap on their pledges, these acts are already proscribed:

- Requiring pledges to ingest alcohol in any quantity (One pledge, found dead in a nearby river, turned up a blood-alcohol level that registered at autopsy as four times the legal limit. Some universities are seriously considering the "dry" option.)

- Requiring pledges to submit to branding or marking of any type

- Requiring pledges to submit to force-feeding of foods or any unwanted substance

- Requiring pledges to perform intense calisthenics (A pledge

---

## Written on the Wall

Charisma Carpenter and Greg Vaughan must be wondering if they're already fighting on-camera stereotypes! Despite these actors' relatively brief careers, they've appeared together on both *Malibu Shores* and *Buffy the Vampire Slayer.* In both instances they've portrayed a couple engaged in a fleeting romance!

\* \* \*

admitted to the ER of his local hospital in cardiac arrest had been forced to complete *2,500* push-ups.)

- Requiring pledges to submit to "swatting," "paddling," or any other physical abuse

- Requiring pledges to submit to physical confinement (One young man asphyxiated after spending seven hours with his hands and ankles tied together behind his back; another nearly died of oxygen deprivation after being confined for an entire night in a dog kennel intended for housing a dog weighing only sixty pounds.)

- Requiring pledges to submit themselves to exposure to cold, heat, or other extreme environmental factors, either within or outside the fraternity house

- Requiring pledges to find their way home after being dumped in an unknown location

While few or no thoughts about these acts immediately flashed through the audience's minds as Xander was paddled and dressed in women's clothing, they most certainly did after the credits rolled. And isn't the ability to linger in a viewer's mind after the TV is turned off the real mark of a program's mastery of the medium, its capability to touch us?

# EPISODE:

# "Halloween"

the short version

Everyone needs a healthy fantasy life, but the role-playing turns way too real for Buffy and the Slayerettes when an old "friend" of Giles's curses them so that they become the characters depicted by their Halloween costumes! While Buffy faints and screams on cue as a period noblewoman, Xander crawls through the bushes as Sunnydale's version of Rambo, and Willow literally looses touch with herself when she rises from her body as a ghost. Unfortunately, none of these characters is much use against the army of ghouls and monsters the opportunistic Spike suddenly finds at his disposal.

## As American as . . . Halloween?

the long look

Folklorists report an alarming trend developing among today's teens—especially those such as Buffy's California-style crew who have a need to create their own culture daily—a tendency to view everything pre-Nintendo as "ancient" history. "They create language—like 'wiggins'—and styles in clothes or body art or even decor; grunge is still popular, I think—but as soon as they create it, it's dated!" So says Peter Walkins, currently studying the remnants of Cornish language and history in Newfoundland. He laughs as one of the many schoolkids

## QUESTIONS

1. **Which actor appeared under his own name in this episode?**

   A. Larry Bagby

   B. Eric Saiet

   C. Robin Sachs

   D. Danny Strong

2. **Which of the following was never a working title for any of the *Halloween* series of horror films?**

   A. *Halloween: The Revenge of Laurie Strode*

   B. *Halloween: The Return of Michael Myers*

   C. *Halloween: Life in the Fast Lane*

   D. *Halloween: Season of the Witch*

3. **Which *Buffy the Vampire Slayer* regular has a real tattoo on his/her back?**

   A. Sarah Michelle Gellar

   B. Alyson Hannigan

   C. Nicholas Brendon

   D. David Boreanaz

4. **What is the name of the druidic feast that falls on the same day as Halloween?**

   A. Sabbat

   B. Samhein

   C. Beltane

   D. Lammas

who follow him about suggests that Cromwell might have had better luck in England if he'd had Hadrian build some more walls. "It's funny, but young people, especially those who are fed names, dates, and events in one long story that educators call 'world history,' seldom realize the huge spans of time involved. After all, in the history book there's only a few dozen pages between the Roman circus and the Battle of Waterloo. It takes a long time for them to fill in all the little blanks that get glossed over in school, for them to grasp

## Who Was That?

**EPISODE PRODUCTION NUMBER: 5V06**

**ORIGINAL AIR DATE: OCTOBER 27, 1997**

**WRITTEN BY: CARL ELLSWORTH**

**DIRECTED BY: BRUCE SETH GREEN**

### CAST

| | |
|---|---|
| Buffy Summers | Sarah Michelle Gellar |
| Xander Harris | Nicholas Brendon |
| Willow Rosenberg | Alyson Hannigan |
| Cordelia Chase | Charisma Carpenter |
| Rupert Giles | Anthony Stewart Head |

### GUEST CAST

| | |
|---|---|
| Angel | David Boreanaz |
| Oz | Seth Green |
| Spike | James Marsters |
| Drusilla | Juliet Landau |
| Principal Snyder | Armin Shimerman |
| Ethan | Robin Sachs |

**Can't blame Oz for being smitten at first sight!**

5. Which of the following isn't the name of a real band?

A. Velvet Chain
B. Four Star Mary
C. Dingoes Ate My Baby
D. Nickel

that the Medieval Era didn't get properly started until a thousand years *after* Hadrian was in his fence-building mode."

It's this lack of what Walkins calls "time-sense" that he believes accounts for the popular notion that Halloween is some ancient custom that was merely dusted off and appropriated by the candy companies, a custom that fits rather easily into still more developing myths such as those in *Buffy* itself. "I've had folklore students," Walkin says, "who really should know better after spending all that money on years of history classes, ask me why the Druids carved pumpkins! Because they've heard all these Halloween stories all their lives, they accept them as 'real,' or as real as any history can be, and don't even stop to think that Druids would have had to travel

ANSWERS

1. A

2. C

3. A

4. B

5. C

## Everything I Ever Needed to Know, I Learned from *Buffy*

† This Week's Fashion Lesson:

† Don't substitute slaying for a good hairdresser.

† "A black eye heals, Buffy, but cowardice has an unlimited shelf life."—Xander

† Hey, making your costume isn't such a bad thing— in Sunnydale.

† As Halloween giveaways, toothbrushes definitely fall into the "trick" category.

† Men with muskets rank high on the social scale— if you think it's 1775.

halfway around the world just to find a pumpkin! Pumpkins are New World veggies, and the only Europeans walking these shores contemporaneously with the Druids were the Vikings!"

While perched on a rocky hillside over one of the first settled bays in North America, he counts the "traditional" Halloween figures on one hand. "Jack-o'-lanterns, black cats, Druids, witches, all those candy 'sacrifices' and then, of course, there's the dead—the basic ghosts, skeletons, and in modern times, vampires, though Buffy did get that right. Traditionally, vampires feared Halloween because the souls believed to be free on that night were as hungry and as greedy as the vampires themselves. Now, if we were to really believe there's some continuous series of rituals and events that link all those items into a single, unified Halloween legend we'd have to ignore some important history along the way.

"Jack-o'-lanterns are obviously a relatively 'new' addition to the Halloween tale, coming in somewhere after 1500. Cats, black or otherwise, simply weren't common in Great Britain until 1100, and never in Ireland, which is often cited as the source of this or that Halloween tradition. Finding any reference to any cats at all is so rare that . . . well, I can't think of a single reliable mention of a cat in any folklore that dates back even two hundred years, so I'd have a hard time believing that Druids incorporated them into rituals nearly two *thousand* years old!

"Witches are the bane of a folklorist's life." Shaking his head, he waves a hand toward the numerous tiny communities scattered along the shoreline. "In this one small bay, you'll find Scots, English, Irish, Flemish, Norman, Dutch, and Cornish descendants, all inter-mingled, all harboring some memory of something they once heard someone's grandmother's father's sister say about witches. 'Muddled' is a kind description of the history of 'witches' in Europe. And, with the addition of neopagan ideas, it's impossible to figure out which witch was which. In the Low Countries, a 'witch' was most likely a midwife, not a practitioner of magic. In Wales, certain forms of witchery, petty charms to keep milk fresh and such, appear in a fairly large body of reference materials, but other forms, especially divina-tion, were heavily proscribed. Just getting a definition of 'witch' is practically impossible. Given that, it's even more impossible for a folklorist, or a historian, to credit accounts of witches' sabbat and broomsticks and all the rest—especially when most of the accounts come from those with something definite to gain by simply making up baseless stories! The vampires? A bigger muddle, but absolutely

**Maybe if Xander had written his name on his dogtags, he wouldn't have turned into Rambo, Jr.!**

133

disconnected from Halloween."

So what exactly is Halloween all about?

"That'll depend on who you ask, of course, but from a historical perspective, we know that there definitely was a non-Christian festival on or about October 31 that included elements of thanksgiving for the year's harvest. To call it Wicca or Druidic or part of the Old Religion is probably a misnomer. All agrarian societies celebrated the end of the year's work in the fields, not just those that currently link their harvest festivals with the dead as Halloween does.

"We also know that All Hallows' Day, also known as All Saints' Day, was once celebrated on May 13, but like many 'Christian' festivals, Christmas itself being the most noteworthy, it was moved to a new date that coincided with local custom. Sometime in the seventh century, it shifted to February 21. It became November 1, back in 835. And that's probably when the muddling and mixing of traditions started. Romanization was a slow process; the Romans themselves probably never even made it to Ireland! Christianity wasn't universally adopted, and old practices wouldn't have lost favor overnight. Introducing Janus, a Roman god, was probably more appropriate historically, but who knows Janus?

"A possible scenario—no one knows for sure, of course—but a possible scenario to explain the basis of our modern Halloween could be some combination: the All Hallows' celebration traditionally linked with the dead, the celebrations of the harvest festivals, and the beginning of the Celtic New Year which also began on November 1."

And the trick-or-treaters, the costumes, and the candy?

"Well, even if you aren't willing to put it all down to a canny conspiracy between the confectionery companies to create yet another holiday dependent on sweets, you'll still have to make a big time jump to find any mention of trick-or-treating! It really does seem to have started in the United States. For all the claims that Halloween harkens back to some dark Druidical beginning, you simply won't find kids running up and down London streets in costumes or banging on doors looking for treats! It doesn't happen.

"Over here, however, you'll find dozens of newspaper articles dating back to the 1930s that slowly reveal a holiday more similar to the one we celebrate. Far from a 'tradition,' the 'beggars' night,'

## Written on the Wall

**You'd almost think that a guy with a century or so of experience under his belt would be able to work his VCR, wouldn't you? Well, you'd be wrong. Watch the tape as Spike tells his minion to "rewind" the action. Instead of backing up the tape, the putz zips right along to the climatic-ending shot of Buffy about to drive a signpost through their colleague! Should have hired a high-school kid to run the aud-vid equipment, Spike. Too bad you killed most of the kids in "School Hard," huh?**

\* \* \*

**Willow must be one of the most talented ghosts of all time. Despite telling Giles she couldn't turn the pages of a book in her phantasmic form, she managed to rustle the curtains and *shut the door behind her*!**

\* \* \*

as it was once called, was a well-publicized effort to turn young people's attention away from the high-jinks then associated with Halloween, things like tipping over people's outhouses. In the cities, however, vandalism took on more violent overtones throughout the turn of the century, right up to the Roaring Twenties. Basically, the candy thing was a bribe to keep kids out of trouble. Canadians never really developed a 'Devil's Night' tradition, as the States has done; we just went for the sweets from the beginning!"

So, Halloween really has no history of its own before the 1930s?

"Only inasmuch as most northern cultures, facing a long, usually rough, winter, have always devised rituals and festivals and carnivals to let off a little steam as the dark months closed in. Some of those celebrations had religious overtones; some were pure fun; some, like the American Halloween, were basically political. But that's the thing about history, about folklore: It *isn't* static. We create history every day. It's just rather sad that we can't appreciate it without dressing it up in historic myth–conception."

135

It may not be a career, but the work is definitely steady.

# "Lie to Me"

J ust when Buffy is ready to enjoy the sudden appearance of Billy Fordham—a blast from her past at Hemery High in Los Angeles—Spike and Drusilla seem particularly intent on filling Sunnydale's nights with peril. Oddly enough, though, it's Billy, not Spike and Dru, who sets Angel's fangs on edge. While Buffy can brush off Angel's angst as all-too-human jealousy, Willow and Giles's growing concern is harder to ignore.

the short version

## Vampire Wanna-Be's

Sexy. Seductive. Immortal. Possessed of superhuman strength, responsible to no one, and beyond the bounds of societal taboos, the vampire, despite its horrific nature, titillates the human psyche's need to explore forbidden realms. Vampire fiction includes vampire romances, vampire detectives, even vampire fantasy. Writing about vamps is no longer relegated to just the horror shelves of bookstores. The romanticized vampire combines sex and power with a remoteness, a mystique, that any number of teenage, leather-jacketed young men would envy. Vampires are the ultimate nonconformists, the supreme rebels. If they're also melancholic, angry, fixated on death, attracted to the dark underbelly of urban life, and partial to an all-black wardrobe, well, so are many teens.

the longer look

QUESTIONS

1. Which of the following is
   an acknowledged vampire
   cult?

   A. The Temple of the Sun
   B. The People's Temple
   C. The Salvation Army
   D. The Callax Phalanx

2. Which films featured vampires that could fly?

   A. *The Lost Boys*
   B. *Interview with the
      Vampire*
   C. *Love at First Bite*
   D. *The Night Stalker*

3. Who wasn't a fictional
   vampire slayer?

   A. R. M. Renfield
   B. Captain Kronos
   C. Blade
   D. Abraham Van Helsing

4. Which of these Suther-
   lands has no connection
   to vampire films?

   A. Kristine
   B. Kalvin
   C. Kiefer
   D. Donald

# Who Was That?

**PRODUCTION NUMBER: 5V07**

**ORIGINAL AIR DATE: NOVEMBER 3, 1997**

**WRITTEN BY: JOSS WHEDON**

**DIRECTED BY: JOSS WHEDON**

## CAST

| | |
|---|---|
| Buffy Summers | Sarah Michelle Gellar |
| Xander Harris | Nicholas Brendon |
| Willow Rosenberg | Alyson Hannigan |
| Cordelia Chase | Charisma Carpenter |
| Rupert Giles | Anthony Stewart Head |

## GUEST CAST

| | |
|---|---|
| Angel | David Boreanaz |
| Ms. Jenny Calendar | Robia La Morte |
| Spike | James Marsters |
| Drusilla | Juliet Landau |
| Billy Fordham (Ford) | Jason Behr |
| Marvin Diego | Jarrad Paul |
| Chanterella | Julia Lee |
| James | Will Rothhaar |

The Goth subculture clubs, represented in a downsized version
at Ford's little "club" in "Lie to Me," were the first visible attempt
to ply disaffected youth with Gothic music and atmosphere, and
the chance to act out their dark sides, to let the disenchanted, the
dissenters, and the disenfranchised come out to play. Pancake

makeup made a comeback. The vaguely sadomasochistic aspects of earlier punk movements blossomed in the Goth clubs. Leather, chains, and black silk rubbed up against the heavy brocade gowns of those re-creating the Gothic period's costumes as well as its ambience. (Ford's clique is perhaps most noteworthy for their lousy taste in faux-Goth clothing!) For this group, there could be no more apt symbol than the vampire, and by the time all the disillusioned '60s flower children traded tie-dye for black lace and wandered into the growing number of clubs, new Gothicism was evolving into one of the biggest role-playing games ever, a game where everybody wanted to play the vampire!

As the Goth scene found its way into mainstream consciousness, Sally Jessy Raphaël and her ilk dragged the truly fringe element back into the daylight to highlight their Halloween specials and shock the nation with the "discovery" that a minuscule number of Gothic enthusiasts had forgotten where the line between fantasy and reality belonged. While most clubbers viewed their night on the town as nothing more than the chance to leave the kids with the sitter and let the *parents* play dress-up, "vampire cultists" were making the news with their claims of bloodsucking as recreation. Televisions in hundreds of barbershops and beauty salons tuned in

5. Who is the only actor who has to *remove* pointy teeth before starting work on *Buffy the Vampire Slayer*?

A. Anthony Stewart Head
B. Armin Shimerman
C. Kristine Sutherland
D. Robia La Morte

## Everything I Ever Needed to Know, I Learned from *Buffy*

† Jealousy and suspicion aren't *always* bad.

† New guys never like old guys.

† The adage "cold hands, warm heart" doesn't really apply to vampires.

† Beat his Slayer, threaten his girl, but don't ever steal a Watcher's books!

† They don't make angry mobs like they used to.

† "Check the lock" takes on new meanings inside a cage.

139

**ANSWERS**

**1. D**

**2. A, B, and C**

**3. A**

**4. B**

**5. B**

to an interview with "Lothella." As the bleached-blond teenager with her black lipstick and studded tongue detailed the mutual bloodsucking that had accompanied her latest roll in the hay, women in rollers nodded sagely under their dryers when the interviewer suggested Lothella see an exorcist. Oddly enough, no one proposed she see a good shrink first!

A murder wrapped in New Goth trappings further polarized the country. The later admission that the murdering kids had "thought they'd get off easy for insanity" if they styled their killing after some vampiric rite barely made a blip in the papers that had screamed, *VAMPIRE ATTACK!* just months ago.

The Gothic fascination with death, easily observed after walking through a Goth club full of black-shrouded figures with their bone-white faces and blackened eyes, however, permeates not only the atmosphere of the movement, but the psyche of many of its younger adherents. Psychologists tell us eight out of every ten teens fantasize about suicide. The vast majority never progress beyond the revenge imagery of their devastated families sobbing around a coffin. The "You'd be sorry if I killed myself" fantasy, however, is seldom carried to its obvious conclusion—that only *dead* people end up in coffins in the first place! It's this mental immaturity that usually characterizes teen contemplations of suicide. Thankfully, few are so truly traumatized or depressed to feel suicide is their best or only option. Even fewer would, as Ford did, see vampirism as a path to immortality.

One psychologist of adolescents, Maire Winter, actually applauds the Goths' obsession with death: "In a society that never discusses its deepest fears, playing with all this Goth paraphernalia allows some people to act out their death fears and fantasies and then put all their toys and costumes back in the closet. The sexual overtones common to Gothic role-playing is, likewise, a relatively safe outlet for sexual expression. It's sort of like the *Buffy* show itself, fun for a few hours, a chance to play with fear, like a roller coaster. People who bring their fantasies into the open are the least likely to act them out in self-destructive ways."

Peter Halling, one of Winter's California colleagues, isn't so sure. "Winter's clients, for all their 'bad girl' or 'bad boy' attitudes, come from relatively stable homes. Not all these kids do. You take a kid

**What teenage Goth fans like Chanterella have on their dressers instead of perfume.**

who's been streeting it since she was eleven, hooking since she was twelve, and for whom S and M isn't some sexual fantasy but a reality that leaves her battered and bruised three times a night for the sake of the sixty bucks she'll split fifty-fifty with whoever's 'protecting' her that week, and, well, the Goth scene's not a playground anymore."

Halling, who worked in southern Miami for twelve of the Goth movement's most prolific years, identifies strongly with the fictional kids from "Lie to Me." "Yeah, there really are Chanterellas out there. Young men and young women so disenfranchised that any experience, even death, seems an improvement. When the subculture's trappings fail to provide enough of an escape, some will step fully into the fantasy, and wherever there's that depth of vulnerability, there'll be someone to take advantage of it. And there's no Buffy to save them."

## Written on the Wall

The camera lens is a thin barrier these days. Just a few weeks before Anthony Stewart Head announced his hope to direct several upcoming third-season episodes, Todd McIntosh, a makeup supervisor working on the show, stepped in front of the camera. He was the "vampire" who greeted Willow with a bright "Hi!" as she, Xander, and Giles passed his coffin on their way into the makeshift bomb-shelter club.

\* \* \*

The antics of Count Dracula have been immortalized in more than seventy different films. Some, like the satirically named and X-rated *Intercourse with the Vampire,* are only marginally related to Bram Stoker's tale, but the version Billy Fordham, Ford to his former friends, knows by heart is considerably more traditional. This one stars Jack Palance as the evil Count in the more stodgily named 1973 film *Dracula.*

\* \* \*

**If Giles had known what sort of Slayer he would end up watching, he might well have stayed on the other side of the Pond, where the Bay City Rollers were society's biggest horror!**

# "The Dark Age"

the short version

Giles's past haunts him—and everyone else in Sunnydale, when a demon starts killing off the university chums of Giles's misspent youth and then decides to holiday on the Hellmouth, bringing with it yet more trouble for the Slayerettes. With Giles's decisions made suspect by his personal involvement—and some serious guilt—Buffy and the others attempt to fill the knowledge gap—with varying degrees of success.

## When It's Hard to Get Your Z's

the longer look

For most people, a cozy bed covered with layers of smooth cotton sheets and fluffy pillows is the perfect end to a long day. Dreams, the harmless escapism of our unconscious minds, are nothing more than pleasant diversions that float away almost before our lashes flutter open each morning. Nightmares, even the ones that leave you trembling and groping for light switches, quickly fade from memory, too. At least, for most people. Anyone watching *Buffy the Vampire Slayer* on a regular basis, however, knows Buffyverse dreams operate on an entirely different plane, that of startling premonitions. In Sunnydale, dreams—and nightmares—usually come true.

When the series opened with "Welcome to the Hellmouth," the Master's imminent arrival sent shockwaves through Buffy's

# Who Was That?

EPISODE PRODUCTION NUMBER: 5V08

ORIGINAL AIR DATE: NOVEMBER 10, 1997

WRITTEN BY: DEAN BATALI AND ROB DES HOTEL

DIRECTED BY: BRUCE SETH GREEN

## CAST

| | |
|---|---|
| Buffy Summers | Sarah Michelle Gellar |
| Xander Harris | Nicholas Brendon |
| Willow Rosenberg | Alyson Hannigan |
| Cordelia Chase | Charisma Carpenter |
| Rupert Giles | Anthony Stewart Head |
| Angel | David Boreanaz |

## GUEST CAST

| | |
|---|---|
| Ms. Jenny Calendar | Robia La Morte |
| Ethan Rayne | Robin Sachs |
| Dierdre Page | Wendy Way |
| Philip Henry | Stuart McLean |
| Detective Winslow | Carlease Burke |
| Custodian | Michael Earl Reid |
| Morgue Attendant | Tony Sears |
| Creepy Cult Guy | Daniel Henry Murray |
| Man | John Bellucci |

dreams. While vampires might be the natural stuff of a Slayer's nightmares, these visions weren't simply bad dreams of vague dangers. Buffy dreamed in intimate—and accurate—detail of specific places, events, and, for want of a better term, "people" she'd never previously encountered. Sort of defines premonitory dreaming, huh? And it's not just Sunnydale's Slayer who gets flashes of the future. As "The Dark Age" makes plain, so do Watchers.

Oddly enough, amid the demons and the vampires, the invisible people and the werewolves, these little psychical forecasts seem almost, well, normal. While that might be a matter of relativity— the premonitions being relatively less bizarre than, say, a teacher who turns into a huge praying mantis—the lack of comment about Buffy's and Giles's dream-time activity may have something to do with an unconscious degree of acceptance, even belief, on the part of the audience. Premonitions that are startlingly accurate are reported almost every day under reliable circumstances.

Of all premonitions, those of death and high tragedy are the ones most likely to be commented on, remembered, and recorded. The story of Mary Matthews, who refused to board the *Titanic* after a premonitory dream, is recorded in a dated letter sent to her mother. "Though it's probably the height of foolishness and I shall no doubt regret missing the opportunity to sail aboard this magnificent vessel, the dreams of the past week have been so vivid, with

---

## Everything I Ever Needed to Know, I Learned from *Buffy*

† The police don't make social calls—even to unassuming, presumably boring, librarians.

† School + Saturday = A Bad Thing

† Never turn your back on a man who sells cursed Halloween costumes.

† Decapitation isn't a cure for anything.

# SLAYER-IN-TRAINING TRIVIA

## QUESTIONS

1. Which of the following isn't an actual mystical order?

   A. The Hermetic Order of the Golden Dawn
   B. The Ancient and Mystical Order of the Rosy Cross
   C. The Praiseworthy and Mystical Order of Eygone
   D. The Order of the Cubic Stone

2. What do Robin Beauchesne, Michael F. Blake, Alan Friedman, Dayne Johnson, Margie Latinopoulos, John Maldonado, Todd McIntosh, Brigette A. Myre, Gerald Quist, Craig Reardon, Mark Shostrom, John Vulich, and John Wheaton all have in common?

   A. They were all awarded an Emmy for "Outstanding Makeup for a Series" while working on *Buffy the Vampire Slayer.*
   B. They were all staked on-screen.
   C. They provided the background screams for *Buffy the Vampire Slayer.*
   D. They created the "vampire dust" graphics for *Buffy the Vampire Slayer.*

Hard to believe the Man in Tweed ever rocked or rolled.

me even as I write this, that I cannot place my foot upon the gangplank without such fear as would spoil the trip for me in any case. Mother, I suspect you and I shall laugh about this when I finally do arrive. . . ." Needless to say, no one was laughing three weeks later when the unsinkable ship sank.

William Stead certainly wasn't laughing either as the icy water washed across the deck. Ten years prior to his ill-fated crossing, Stead, a novelist and journalist, wrote *Crossing*, a tale about a super ship he named *Majestic* striking an iceberg. The uncanny similarity between the real events and the fictional ones did wonders for sales of *Crossing*, but didn't help Stead avoid drowning.

146

President Abraham Lincoln's premonitions about his own death might have been nothing more than the usual worry of a public official who carries out some unpopular policies except *he wasn't the only one to foresee it!* Charles Dickens, Margaret Summer-Stead, Gail Crowell, and Percival Altman-Clarke all recorded their dreams through their letters. From Summer-Stead, "I fear our good President shall not last out the term. My dreams show him at the height of his power, surrounded by crowds from which will emerge a single angry soul who will fire a lone bullet and end our Union's hope." From Crowell's correspondence, dated the same day as Summer-Stead's, "Such horrid visions, of Lincoln's bloodied figure lying at the feet of a great crowd, that I cannot sleep for fear that, in some way, my dreaming shall make it all too real."

Lincoln's own dreams were less detailed about the circumstances of his death, though he felt sure it would be violent, and he described his recurring dream this way: "I am on a deep, broad, rolling river; I am in a boat, and I am falling in! I am falling in!" Other aspects of his death were crystal clear. "A great crowd of people walks through the White House, surrounding a coffin, and in that coffin, I am laid out in the new suit and a collar that nips."

What makes Buffy's dreams, and Giles's as well, different from Dickens's or Stead's are the Slayer's and the Watcher's dream *sources.* Most people who believe in predictive dreams, dreams that seem fated to play out in real life, feel that they have evolved some innate ability to add up tiny clues that lead to inevitable conclusions, which get expressed as dreams, or that some sort of guardian angel whispers in the ears of those capable of listening. Neither scenario fits the Buffyverse events. Giles's visions linked him to the actions of a demon and a madman—not angels. There were no clues to link, no conclusions to draw. Nothing in the normal world could lead to Giles's *detailed* visions! Buffy's numerous nocturnal revelations have revolved around vampires, demons inhabiting stolen bodies. No unconscious hints could predict her mother's exact words or that she'd destroy crockery. The obvious suggestion, that this Slayer and her Watcher are irrevocably linked to other things, the things they hate most, might well keep them up at night.

3. **Who was born May 20, 1956?**

   A. Ken Lerner
   B. James Marsters
   C. David Boreanaz
   D. Dean Butler

4. **Which actor paid real money to sing about transvestites on stage?**

   A. Robin Sachs
   B. Robia La Morte
   C. David Boreanaz
   D. Anthony Stewart Head

5. **Which actor's real-life tattoo is a Chinese character?**

   A. David Boreanaz
   B. Sarah Michelle Gellar
   C. Robia La Morte
   D. Anthony Stewart Head

**ANSWERS**

1. C

2. A

3. D

4. D

5. B

# Written on the Wall

For American high-school students, Xander and Buffy have some mighty exotic tastes in fantasy lovers. Xander's got the hots for Amy Yipp, better known for her silicon implants than her acting ability; she is the Pamela Anderson Lee of Hong Kong. And Buffy's into Gavin Rossdale, lead singer and swanky songwriter of the British band Bush, who probably floats through the minds of a very select subset of British teens, but an American junior certainly makes for an odd groupie.

\* \* \*

Though broad comedy is a *Buffy* hallmark, the more subtle ironies are also pretty well represented, as in the "Very good. The rest is silence" quote uttered by Giles when Buffy finally gives up her aerobicizing antics in the library. A line from *Hamlet,* it's totally appropriate to our favorite Brit, but it's also the same line that foreshadowed the death of Merrick, Buffy's first Watcher, in the original *Buffy the Vampire Slayer* film.

\* \* \*

Hmmm? How exactly did Cordelia know the police were investigating a homicide? She wasn't in the library for the first part of Giles's encounter with Detective Winslow, and it's difficult to picture Giles engaging in deeply personal discussions while Cordelia continues trying to get her traffic ticket fixed. So, how did she know? Who told her?

\* \* \*

Oops! Giles must have been away from home for too long. He's obviously forgotten how to calculate the time difference between California and England. According to the clock on the wall, Giles made his call to Dierdre Page at a quarter to three. Yet, when he glances at his wristwatch and does his mental calculations, he deduces it must be 5:00 A.M. in London! Only if they moved California to the Azores!

\* \* \*

148

EPISODE:

# "What's My Line?"

## (Parts 1 and 2)

**P**art 1:  Career Day holds no anticipation, no mystery for Buffy. Her destiny as the Slayer is preordained, her choices limited. Willow is wooed by some mysterious computer company geeks; Xander prepares to investigate his bright future in Institutionalized Corrections; and Cordelia is trying to decide between the professions of personal shopping and inspirational speaking. Meanwhile Buffy, Angel, and Giles attempt to fend off an unending line of assassins long enough to find out just why Spike and Drusilla are robbing libraries and graves! Phew! Busy day.

**Part 2**:  Buffy's future looks considerably different when another "buff" young woman appears and puts a serious kink in the whole Slayer mythology by introducing herself as Kendra *the Vampire Slayer*! Like Buffy needed an identity crisis? Like she didn't have enough to do just ducking the overachieving Order of Taraka, discovering how Spike and Drusilla planned to restore Dru to full health, and keeping her boyfriend alive? It's enough to make even the most dedicated Slayer consider early retirement!

## When I Grow Up, I Wanna Be . . .

In kindergarten classes, half the boys want to be cops, half the girls want to be nurses. By elementary school, a quarter of the boys want to be astronauts, the girls want to be archaeolo-

the short version

the longer look

149

# Who Was That?

EPISODE PRODUCTION NUMBERS: PART 1, 5V09
  PART 2, 5V10

ORIGINAL AIR DATES: PART 1, NOVEMBER 17, 1997
  PART 2, NOVEMBER 21, 1997

WRITTEN BY: PART 1, HOWARD GORDON AND MARTI NOXON
  PART 2, MARTI NOXON

DIRECTED BY: PART 1, DAVID SOLOMON
  PART 2, DAVID SEMEL

---

## CAST (PART 1)

| | |
|---|---|
| Buffy Summers | Sarah Michelle Gellar |
| Xander Harris | Nicholas Brendon |
| Willow Rosenberg | Alyson Hannigan |
| Cordelia Chase | Charisma Carpenter |
| Rupert Giles | Anthony Stewart Head |

## GUEST CAST

| | |
|---|---|
| Angel | David Boreanaz |
| Spike | James Marsters |
| Drusilla | Juliet Landau |
| Oz | Seth Green |
| Principal Snyder | Armin Shimerman |
| Dalton | Eric Saiet |
| Kendra | Bianca Lawson |
| Norman Pfister | Kelly Connell |
| First Assassin | Uncredited |
| Suitman | Michael Rothhaar |
| Mrs. Kalish | P. B. Hutton |

## CAST (PART 2)

| | |
|---|---|
| Buffy Summers | Sarah Michelle Gellar |
| Xander Harris | Nicholas Brendon |
| Willow Rosenberg | Alyson Hannigan |
| Cordelia Chase | Charisma Carpenter |
| Rupert Giles | Anthony Stewart Head |

## GUEST CAST

| | |
|---|---|
| Angel | David Boreanaz |
| Spike | James Marsters |
| Drusilla | Juliet Landau |
| Oz | Seth Green |
| Kendra | Bianca Lawson |
| Willy | Saverio Guerra |
| Hostage Kid | Danny Strong |
| Patrice | Spice Williams |

gists, and their parents are delighted if they don't have any budding Sunday-night wrestlers or bass guitarists in their midst. It's a fact of life that 90 percent of parents want their kids to be doctors, lawyers, or accountants, while those same kids find those options gross or boring. It's a pretty safe bet though that, even if Richard Dawson was doing the polling, no one would want their beautiful seventeen-year-old daughter to spend her nights crawling through cemeteries with her hip pocket full of sharp, pointy objects! (Hey, even Buffy knows a dead-end job when she sees one!)

With parents pushing the doctor-lawyer-accountant line, and teens pushing right back, it seems almost inevitable that computers become the final arbiters of aptitude, that humanity's completely emotionless creation should decide the fate of its children. In some

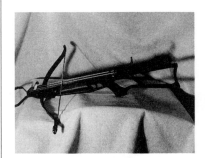

**The natural weapon of all evil-vamp hunters.**

### QUESTIONS

1. **Which actress appeared with her father in *Ed Wood*?**

   A. Julie Benz
   B. Juliet Landau
   C. Bianca Lawson
   D. Robia La Morte

2. **Who won an Emmy for "Outstanding Music Composition for a Series (Dramatic Underscore)" in 1998?**

   A. Seth Green
   B. Joss Whedon
   C. Christophe Beck
   D. Nerf Herder

3. **Who contributed a voice cameo to *Buffy the Vampire Slayer*?**

   A. Joss Whedon
   B. Alfred Hitchcock
   C. Stephen J. Cannell
   D. Chris Carter

4. **Who was born August 21, 1961?**

   A. Anthony Stewart Head
   B. Armin Shimerman
   C. David Boreanaz
   D. James Marsters

## Everything I Ever Needed to Know, I Learned from *Buffy*

† **Never trust a vamp who reads.**

† **Skate blades make good professional sense, too— if you're a Slayer.**

† **Never give up your day job.**

† **Religion is weird.**

† **Never assume you're irreplaceable.**

† **Messing with a Slayer's boyfriend is a surefire way to piss her off.**

schools, career testing begins in sixth grade, with students being shifted from the sciences to the humanities and back on the advice of a machine that will be obsolete before the kids can memorize their locker combinations! No wonder Xander felt no great loyalty to the corrections career his check marks turned up.

Luckily, most aptitude tests don't suggest participants become landscapers on the strength of a single question about the respondent's fondness for bushes. Some tests, especially those incorporating personality traits into their calculations, can actually turn up some eerily appropriate results. Pro Plus, a commonly administered (well, it's free, what do you expect?) program turned up career suggestions of "Artist" for Van Gogh, "Administrator" for Ronald Reagan, "Army Officer" for Colin Powell, and "Musician" for Rod Stewart. Oddly enough, "Slayer" isn't one of the program's available options, but, based on best-guess responses to the following list of questions, it did spit out "Rescue Worker" and, surprise, surprise, "Law Enforcement Officer," when the program's creators slid the No. 2–penciled responses back into the system.

What about you? Are you a Slayer or a Slayerette? Check *one* answer to each question.

1. Are you most often attracted to:

   (   ) traditional thinkers

   (   ) imaginative thinkers•

2. In approaching others, you prefer to keep conversation:

   (   ) personal•

   (   ) objective

3. You prefer your personal affairs be:

   (   ) settled and decided

   (   ) unsettled and undecided•

4. Within your peer group, are you:

   (   ) up on all the gossip•

   (   ) the one who says, "What?!" when others mention week-old happenings

5. You're more attracted to:

   (   ) spirited argument•

   (   ) harmony of opinion

6. You are more likely to:

   (   ) start conversations•

   (   ) wait for others to begin conversations

7. You handle everyday tasks and events:

   (   ) traditionally

   (   ) experimentally•

8. If a starving boy stole a loaf of bread for his starving mother, you'd judge:

   (   ) according to the law, not specific circumstances

   (   ) according to the specific circumstances, not to the law•

9. In arguments, you are drawn to:

   (   ) convincing facts

   (   ) emotional factors•

10. Are you more:

    (   ) realistic than speculative

    (   ) speculative than realistic•

11. Do you prefer your work schedule to have:

    (   ) clearly demarked deadlines and objectives

    (   ) looser, more self-directed, timing•

12. Would you prefer to:

    (   ) have your head in the clouds•

    (   ) be in a comfortable rut

13. On the phone, do you:

    (   ) improvise•

    (   ) rehearse your requests

14. During an evening out, do you:

    (   ) hate to leave when the evening's over•

    (   ) tire quickly and prefer to go home

15. On a personal level, you are more impressed by another's:

    (   ) principles

    (   ) emotional responses•

**5. Which TV producer *didn't* create a vampire series?**

**A. Dan Curtis**

**B. James Parriot**

**C. Aaron Spelling**

**D. Stephen J. Cannell**

**ANSWERS**

**1. B**

**2. C**

**3. A**

**4. D**

**5. D**

16. During an evening out, you:

( ) mix freely with many people

( ) prefer to mix with a select, well-known group•

17. You make decisions:

( ) impulsively•

( ) carefully

18. During your off hours, you are:

( ) leisurely•

( ) punctual

19. You are more interested in:

( ) the actual

( ) the possible•

20. Given a self-assigned task, you prefer:

( ) starting

( ) finishing•

If nothing else, answering these questions for the regular cast of *Buffy the Vampire Slayer* illustrates the extraordinary efforts that have gone into creating viable, three-dimensional, and internally consistent characters. No wonder everyone secretly loves Willow.

Where do you fall on that character spectrum? Well, the more answers with (•) you chose, the more Slayer-like you are; the fewer, the more Willowesque you'd be. Xander, for example, is more Willowish; Cordelia, perhaps surprisingly, is more like Buffy than either would care to admit.

**Kinda like a mirror—but not, ya know?**

154

**Crypts are for the dead—not dates. Next question?**

**Vampires are as hard on churches as Slayers are on gyms!**

Oops. Buffy's window, the one she comes through even when her mother isn't home, must be magic. When she arrives back to find Angel hugging her pig, the shade is up. No one closes it, but when she sits on the edge of the bed with him, the shade is down—at least in that shot! Without either Angel or Buffy moving, Buffy looks in her mirror and comments on how weird it is to see herself, but no Angel. Guess that's why she didn't notice that the shade was up in the mirror, but down when she turned away.

* * *

Uh-oh. Another of those "Where did it go?" moments. Watch the first assassin get off the bus. See all those *Watch Your Step* signs? Now, check out the next shot of the bus. The signs are gone and the steps have changed color! Clearly two different buses were used for those twenty seconds of scene time. Total time for the Maggot Man's arm to change from its wormy state to a human-seeming appendage: less than ten seconds. Yet, in even that short scene, Maggot Man's sleeve changes length *three* times! More things disappear in "What's My Line?" Part 2, when Xander squashes part of Maggot Man inside a biology book (nice touch), but before Xander can slouch into the nearest chair, the book (and presumably the bug) simply disappears from the table!

* * *

Everyone, even Buffy, has heard of the decoder rings made famous by Captain Midnight and others. Oddly enough, no one is actually sure there ever was a Captain Midnight Decoder Ring!

* * *

This is the first episode where a certain *claddagh* ring, made infamous in "Surprise," is noticeable on Angel's hand. For the curious, it faces in.

* * *

Talk about continuity problems! In the final, climatic scene of "What's My Line?" Part 1, Kendra completes a pretty credible body slam, whacking our favorite Slayer into Angel's coffee table, which shatters into its component pieces right on schedule. Unfortunately, before Buffy is even back on her feet, the table disappears! Subsequent shots continue to show a completely clean floor!

\* \* \*

How did Kendra, newly arrived in town, know where Angel lived?

\* \* \*

Timing is everything, especially if you're trying to re-create a ritual that hasn't been enacted in a vampire's age. So, after waiting all that time, you'd expect everyone involved to keep an eye on the clock, right? Or at least on the sky, in this case. Then why did Giles say the ritual was due on the "new moon" while Spike insisted it was on the night of the "full moon"?

\* \* \*

Why didn't the holy water that set Angel screaming bother Dru as she rubbed it into his chest with her bare fingers?

\* \* \*

"BACK OFF, PINK RANGER!"
Definitely an in-joke here. Buffy's stunt double, Sophia Crawford, also doubled for Pink Ranger in the Power Rangers movie.

\* \* \*

**Hardly responsible parent material anyway!**

# EPISODE:
# "Ted"

Ted is Joyce's perfect man. He's smart, financially secure, even attractive in a parents'-generation kind of way. He pays for miniature golf, hands out free software to all Buffy's friends, and whips up the best mini-pizzas and cookies. He's absolutely ideal—if you don't mind your potential stepfather rummaging through your diary, threatening you, or slapping you around! With everyone, including her friends, her Watcher, and her mother, convinced she's having "parental issues," there's no way anyone will ever believe Buffy didn't *really* try to kill Ted.

the short version

## The Death Toll

Many fans were startled by Buffy's powerful reaction to Ted's first death, not realizing how much depth Whedon and company had built into this character. Far from a killing machine, Buffy Summers remains the angst-ridden teen first introduced in the feature film, and it's this facet of hers, even more than her short skirts and sassy dialogue, that will make her an intriguing and viable character for many seasons.

Of course, that doesn't change the fact that she *does* stake an awful lot of vampires!

the longer look

159

## "WELCOME TO THE HELLMOUTH" (PART 1) "THE HARVEST" (PART 2) TOTAL 7

| KILLEE | KILLER | METHOD |
|---|---|---|
| Victim 1: Anonymous Boy | Darla | She bit him! |
| Victim 2: Jesse | The Master/Xander and Anonymous Girl | He bit him./She pushed Vamp Jesse on Xander's improvised stake. |
| Victim 3: Bronze Bouncer | Luke | Usual vampire suckfest |
| Victim 4: Anonymous Blond Girl | Luke | Sucked dry |
| Victim 5: Anonymous Vamp 1 | Buffy | Staked with pool stick |
| Victim 6: Anonymous Vamp 2 | Buffy | Decapitated with cymbal |
| Victim 7: Luke | Buffy | Staked in the back |

If the numbers for this episode seem high, remember it *was* a two-hour special.

## "THE WITCH" TOTAL 1

Though no one was staked, slashed, or stabbed to death in this episode, and it's entirely possible that Mrs. Madison is very much alive *somewhere,* it's probably safe to conclude she's dead to *this* world! Determining who killed her is a bit complex though. Giles handled the invocation, Buffy beat on her at every opportunity, but the spell that knocked her into a trophy statue was actually cast by Mrs. Madison herself! So, what do you call that? Suicide by magic?

## "TEACHER'S PET" TOTAL 3

| KILLEE | KILLER | METHOD |
|---|---|---|
| Victim 1: Teacher, Dr. Gregory | She-Mantis | Decapitated |
| Victim 2: Anonymous | Buffy | Stabbed with a fence picket |

| | | |
|---|---|---|
| Victim 3: Ms. French, She-Mantis | Buffy | Sliced and diced with big knife |

Unfortunately, Xander can't count fantasy kills like the one in the teaser of "Teacher's Pet"—or fantasy kisses for that matter.

## "NEVER KILL A BOY ON THE FIRST DATE" TOTAL 6

| KILLEE | KILLER | METHOD |
|---|---|---|
| Victim 1: Anonymous Vamp 1 | Buffy | Staked at the graveyard |
| Victims 2–6: Five Bus Passengers | Anonymous Vamps | The usual biting, sucking thing |
| Victim 4: Bus-Passenger Vamp | Buffy | Slides him into morgue incinerator (This is his second death.) |

## "THE PACK" TOTAL 2

| KILLEE | KILLER | METHOD |
|---|---|---|
| Victim 1: A Pig | Xander and the Pack | They ate him |
| Victim 2: Principal Flutie | The Pack | They ate him, too |

## "ANGEL" TOTAL 0

Absolutely no one died in this episode!

## "I, ROBOT—YOU, JANE" TOTAL 2

| KILLEE | KILLER | METHOD |
|---|---|---|
| Victim 1: Dave | Fritz | Hanging, made to appear as suicide |
| Victim 2: Fritz | Moloch | Neck snapped |

## "The Puppet Show" Total 4

| KILLEE | KILLER | METHOD |
|---|---|---|
| Victim 1: Emily the Dancer | Demon, a.k.a. Marc | Heart ripped out |
| Victim 2: Morgan | Demon, a.k.a. Marc | Brain ripped out |
| Victim 3: Sid | Sid, Demon-hunter | Suicide via demon slayage |
| Victim 4: Demon, a.k.a. Marc/Xander | Sid, Demon-hunter | Stabbed through the heart/Guillotined |

A regular statistician would have trouble with this episode, but the Buffyverse rules make it perfectly reasonable to have two different people kill the same demon and to have Sid's slaying of the demon qualify as suicide. Weird, huh?

## "Nightmares" Total 0

Figuring out what counts in a "dream episode" of *Buffy the Vampire Slayer* is no easier than figuring out if *Dallas*'s Bobby was really dead or if Pam just dreamed it. As everything went back to "the way it was," no one died permanently, but in the nightmares, specifically in Giles's nightmare, Buffy died in 1997.

## "Invisible Girl," a.k.a. "Out of Sight, Out of Mind" Total 0

This episode had real "killer" potential. Marcie Ross had no way of knowing that Harmony *wouldn't* break her neck falling down that stone staircase, or that Mitch's skull was thick enough to withstand her flailing at it with a baseball bat, or that Buffy would survive being thrown through a ceiling! It's a virtual certainty that Marcie had no intention of rescuing Rupert, Willow, and Xander from the gas-filled boiler room. No, pure luck is all that prevented Marcie Ross from becoming a multiple murderer!

## "PROPHECY GIRL" TOTAL 8

| KILLEE | KILLER | METHOD |
|---|---|---|
| Victim 1: Anonymous Vamp 1 | Buffy | Staked him, of course |
| Victims 2–5: Kevin/Three of the Audiovisual Club | Anonymous Vamps | Standard vampire attack |
| Victim 6: Buffy | The Master | Drowned |
| Victim 7: Anonymous Vamp 2 | Angel | Staked him, of course |
| Victim 8: The Master | Buffy | Dropped him on the mother of all stakes |

Just as a side note, although we're only counting on-screen kills here, when Buffy offed Anonymous Vamp #1 in the opening teaser, she indicated it was the third vamp of the night, so she'd already made away with two others before we hit the opening credits!

Before the bean-counting fans start quibbling over the total dead in this episode, Kendra's appearance in later episodes is a pretty sure indication that Buffy was indeed dead, even if she was just "technically" dead.

## Everything I Ever Needed to Know, I Learned from *Buffy*

† Mini golf just isn't a life-lesson situation.

† Never take candies—or cookies—from strangers who want to date your mother.

† Killing your mother's beau is a sure path to serious grounding.

† Given the right set of circumstances, a nail file is as handy as a stake.

† If sparks start flying, literally, when you kiss, stop kissing.

† Tweed could save law enforcement a fortune!

## "WHEN SHE WAS BAD" TOTAL 6

| KILLEE | KILLER | METHOD |
|---|---|---|
| Victim 1: Anonymous Vamp 1 | Buffy | Tossed onto a broken tree branch |
| Victim 2: Anonymous Vamp 2 | Buffy | Staked from behind |
| Victim 3: Anonymous Female Vamp 3 | Buffy | Staked |
| Victim 4: Anonymous Vamp 4 | Angel | Staked |
| Victim 5: Anonymous Vamp 5 | Buffy | Staked with a pole |
| Victim 6: Absalom, Vamp 6 | Buffy | Burnt |

Unique body count here! Dead Vamps, 6; Dead Humans, 0.

It's also the quickest set of kills to date, five vampires in about five minutes!

## "SOME ASSEMBLY REQUIRED" TOTAL 1

| KILLEE | KILLER | METHOD |
|---|---|---|
| Victim 1: Vamp 1, Mr. Corshack | Buffy | Staked with a shovel handle |

Of course, the body count would be higher by three if we included the girls who died in the car crash before the action of "Some Assembly Required" began. We'll eliminate Daryl from the total, too. Sure he died, but he was also brought back to life once, so if you look at the sum of living and dying, he's sort of a zero.

## "SCHOOL HARD" TOTAL 9

| KILLEE | KILLER | METHOD |
|---|---|---|
| Victim 1: Anonymous Vamp 1 | Buffy | Stake to the heart |
| Victims 2–3: "Fish Tank"ers | Spike | Chomp, chomp |
| Victim 4: Sheila | Drusilla | Sucked and vamped |
| Victim 5: Anonymous Teacher 1 | Spike | Broken neck |
| Victim 6: Anonymous Teacher 2 | Anonymous Vamp | Typical vamp attack |
| Victim 7: Anonymous Vamp 2 | Buffy | Staked in the back |
| Victim 8: Anonymous Vamp 3 | Buffy | Staked in the back |
| Victim 9: The Anointed One | Spike | Serious sunburn |

Haven't had this many deaths since the series premiere—and never so many in a single-hour episode!

## "INCA MUMMY GIRL" TOTAL 3

| KILLEE | KILLER | METHOD |
|---|---|---|
| Victim 1: Student, Rodney Munson | Mummy | Kissed to death |
| Victim 2: The real Ampata | Mummy | Killed by a kiss |
| Victim 3: The "bodyguard" | Mummy | Mummified by kiss |

Would Victim 4 be the mummy that called itself Ampata? Depends on your point of view. Sure, she certainly seemed alive, and definitely ended up dead, very dead, but didn't she actually die five hundred years before? And, even if you consider her to be Victim 4, who exactly killed her?

## "REPTILE BOY" TOTAL 0

Considering this whole episode centered on human sacrifice, it's semi-incredible, but completely nice, that absolutely *no one* died!

## "HALLOWEEN" TOTAL 1

| KILLEE | KILLER | METHOD |
|---|---|---|
| Victim 1: Anonymous Vamp 1 | Buffy | Staked with pumpkin-patch sign |

The key to great slayage is to make up for lack of quantity with entertainment value.

## "LIE TO ME" TOTAL 4

| KILLEE | KILLER | METHOD |
|---|---|---|
| Victim 1: Anonymous Vamp 1 | Buffy | Staked |
| Victim 2: Anonymous Vamp 2 | Buffy | Staked |
| Victim 3: Billy Fordham | Spike and Company | Bitten |
| Victim 4: Vamp 3, Billy Fordham | Buffy | Staked |

No, we are not adding Drusilla's dead bird to the list!

## "THE DARK AGE" TOTAL 3

| KILLEE | KILLER | METHOD |
|---|---|---|
| Victim 1: Philip Henry | Eyghon | Strangulation |
| Victim 2: Anonymous Vamp 1 | Buffy | Staked |
| Victim 3: Eyghon | Angel's Demon | Evicted? |

Hmmm, what to do with the reanimated corpses of Dierdre Page and Philip Henry? The *people* who once inhabited those bodies died when Eyghon took over, which is why Philip Henry made the victims list. As Eyghon was hopping from corpse to corpse, however, he didn't actually die when the bodies turned into puddles, so we don't include the dissolution of the corpses as deaths.

## "WHAT'S MY LINE?" PARTS 1 AND 2 TOTAL 6

| KILLEE | KILLER | METHOD |
| --- | --- | --- |
| Victim 1: Anonymous Vamp 1 | Buffy | Staked |
| Victim 2: Mrs. Kalish | Maggot Man | Unknown, but noisy and messy |
| Victim 3: Ugly-Eye Assassin | Buffy | Partial decapitation by skate |
| Victim 4: Anonymous Vamp 2 | Giles | Crossbow bolt to the back |
| Victim 5: Maggot Man | Xander and Charisma | Glued and stomped |
| Victim 6: Anonymous Vamp 3 | Willow and Giles | Staked him |

Though it's most likely that the third assassin died in the church fire, that she didn't survive along with Spike and Dru, . . . until they come up with a body, she doesn't make the list.

## "TED" TOTAL 3

| KILLEE | KILLER | METHOD |
| --- | --- | --- |
| Victim 1: Anonymous Vamp 1 | Buffy | Staked after excessive beating |
| Victim 2: Ted | Buffy | Major disassembly—twice! |
| Victim 3: Anonymous Vamp 2 | Giles | Shoved a crossbow bolt into him, the same one Ms. Calendar had just shot into Giles! |

## "BAD EGGS" TOTAL 6

| KILLEE | KILLER | METHOD |
| --- | --- | --- |
| Victim 1: Vamp, Tector Gorch | Purple Parasite Mom | Unknown, ingestion |

| | | |
|---|---|---|
| Victim 2: Purple Parasite Mom | Buffy | Death by pickax |
| Victim 3: Parasite Baby 1 | Xander | Boiled to death |
| Victim 4: Parasite Baby 2 | Buffy | Stabbed with scissors |
| Victims 5–6: Parasite Babies 3 and 4 | Buffy | Smashed with a toolbox |

You didn't really expect even a rabid fan to count the number of shells that were cracked in this episode, did you?

## "SURPRISE" (PART 1) "INNOCENCE" (PART 2) TOTAL 7

| KILLEE | KILLER | METHOD |
|---|---|---|
| Victim 1: Anonymous Vampire 1 | Buffy | Staked with a piece of wooden truck rail |
| Victim 2: Anonymous Vampire 2 | Buffy | Staked with a drumstick |
| Victim 3: Vampire 3, Dalton | The Judge | Burnt out from the inside |
| Victim 4: Smoking Woman | Angelus | Big bad bite! |
| Victim 5: Jenny's Uncle | Angelus | Messy biting-slicing thing |
| Victim 6: Businessman | The Judge | Burnt out |
| Victim 7: The Judge | Buffy | Blown up by LAWS rocket |

It's tough enough figuring out who killed who in all the shady alleys and half-lit graveyard scenes, so we won't add dream and fantasy killings to our list to further confuse the death-toll list!

## "PHASES" TOTAL 2

| KILLEE | KILLER | METHOD |
|---|---|---|
| Victim 1: Theresa Klusmeyer | Angelus | Standard vamp attack |
| Victim 2: Vampire, Theresa | Xander | Stakes her with an easel |

"Bring 'em back alive" was Buffy's motto for this episode and, in keeping with just that plan, absolutely no one would have died if Angelus had stayed out of the picture!

## "BEWITCHED, BOTHERED, AND BEWILDERED" TOTAL 2

| KILLEE | KILLER | METHOD |
|---|---|---|
| Victim 1: Anonymous Vampire 1 | Buffy | Stake to the heart |
| Victim 2: Quaint Little Shop Girl | Angelus | Ripped her heart out |

## "PASSION" TOTAL 2

| KILLEE | KILLER | METHOD |
|---|---|---|
| Victim 1: Anonymous Girl on Street | Angelus | Bite, bite, bite |
| Victim 2: Jenny Calendar | Angelus | Broken neck |

Yes, Angelus beached and hung four of Willow's fish, but it's tough enough keeping track of the bipeds, okay?

## "KILLED BY DEATH" TOTAL 3

| KILLEE | KILLER | METHOD |
|---|---|---|
| Victim 1: Patient, Tina | Der Kinderstod | Sucked the life out of her |
| Victim 2: Dr. Becker | Der Kinderstod | Slice-and-dice shredding |
| Victim 3: Der Kinderstod | Buffy | Broke his neck |

Although Celia did die, it wasn't a contemporaneous death, so it wasn't included in the death toll.

## "I ONLY HAVE EYES FOR YOU" TOTAL 1

| KILLEE | KILLER | METHOD |
|---|---|---|
| Victim 1: Teacher, Ms. Frank | George | Shot before falling two floors |

Considering this is the first episode to prominently feature handguns, the fact there was only one contemporary death is actually surprising. The average number of gunshot-related deaths in contemporaneous cop shows is almost *five per episode*! James and Grace did die, of course, but despite the number of times their deaths were reenacted, they didn't actually happen during the course of the episode.

## "GO FISH" TOTAL 2

| KILLEE | KILLER | METHOD |
|---|---|---|
| Victim 1: Nurse Greenleigh | Sea Monsters | Unknown, but very messy |
| Victim 2: Coach Marin | Sea Monsters | Unknown, but very . . . you know |

And what about Cameron Walker, Gage Petronzi, Cordy's new fish friend who was once known as Sean, and Dod McAlvy? That's the problem with shows like *Buffy*. Sometimes drawing the line between "dead" and "alive" is tough. If you assume they're themselves, just scalier and with a less fixed address, they don't belong on the list. If you have a different view, take out your felt-tipped marker and scribble away in the margins!

## "BECOMING" (PART 1) "THE WHISTLER" (PART 2) TOTAL 11

| KILLER | KILLEE | METHOD |
|---|---|---|
| Victim 1: Anonymous Vamp 1 | Buffy | The usual staking |
| Victim 2: Anonymous Vamp 2 | Buffy | More staking |
| Victim 3: Museum Curator | Drusilla | Chomp, chomp |
| Victim 4: Anonymous Man | Angelus | Bitten |
| Victim 5: Anonymous Female Vamp 1 | ? | Self-immolation |
| Victim 6: Anonymous Female Vamp 2 | Kendra | Stake to the heart |
| Victim 7: Kendra | Drusilla | Throat slashed |
| Victim 8: Anonymous Vamp 3 | Buffy | Staked |
| Victim 9: Anonymous Vamp 4 | Buffy | Decapitated |
| Victim 10: Anonymous Vamp 5 | Buffy | Straight staking |
| Victim 11: Angel | Buffy | Stabbed and sent to Hell |

### IN FLASHBACKS

| KILLEE | KILLER | METHOD |
|---|---|---|
| Victim 1: Angel | Darla | She sucked his blood, he sucked hers. . . . |

Who *wouldn't* want her for a stepdaughter?

| Victim 2: Priest | Angel | Sucked him dry in the confessional |
| Victim 3: Anonymous Vamp | Buffy | Buffy's first staking |

Okay, so the flashbacks aren't contemporaneous in time with the on-screen action, and they aren't included in the show totals, but as this episode's events were so integral to the program as a whole, they're listed here for your reference convenience.

### QUESTIONS

1. **Which film doesn't feature John Ritter?**
   A. *Bride of Chucky*
   B. *I Woke Up Early the Day I Died*
   C. *Problem Child*
   D. *The Lost Boys*

2. **Which of the following films featured cyborgs?**
   A. *Cyborg*
   B. *Johnny Mnemonic*
   C. *Flatliners*
   D. *RoboCop*

3. **Which actor hasn't played a mechanical man on TV?**
   A. Lee Majors
   B. Brent Spiner
   C. Robert Llewellyn
   D. Rick Springfield

4. **Which program won the Saturn Award for "Best Genre Network Series" in 1998?**
   A. *Buffy the Vampire Slayer*
   B. *The X-Files*
   C. *Space: Above and Beyond*
   D. *Millennium*

5. **Who was born September 17, 1948, in Burbank, California?**
   A. Armin Shimerman
   B. John Ritter
   C. Anthony Stewart Head
   D. Robin Sachs

# Who Was That?

**EPISODE PRODUCTION NUMBER: 5V11**

**ORIGINAL AIR DATE: DECEMBER 8, 1997**

**WRITTEN BY: DAVID GREENWALT AND JOSS WHEDON**

**DIRECTED BY: BRUCE SETH GREEN**

## CAST

| | |
|---|---|
| Buffy Summers | Sarah Michelle Gellar |
| Xander Harris | Nicholas Brendon |
| Willow Rosenberg | Alyson Hannigan |
| Cordelia Chase | Charisma Carpenter |
| Rupert Giles | Anthony Stewart Head |

## GUEST CAST

| | |
|---|---|
| Angel | David Boreanaz |
| Mrs. Joyce Summers | Kristine Sutherland |
| Ms. Jenny Calendar | Robia La Morte |
| Ted Buchanan | John Ritter |
| Detective Stein | James G. MacDonald |
| Neal | Ken Thorley |
| Vampire #1 | Jeff Pruitt |
| Vampire #2 | Jeff Langton |

# Written on the Wall

A quick glance through the credits reveals that Vampire #1, the one Buffy beat the daylights out of with a trash-can lid, was none other than Jeff Pruitt, stunt coordinator for the series. What wasn't so obvious was that, while working out this scene, Pruitt severely bruised his hand and wrist.

\*   \*   \*

Ummm . . . Just where did the miniature-golf course come from? Willow clearly tells us in the season's first episode, "When She Was Bad," that there are no mini-putts in Sunnydale.

\*   \*   \*

Buffy's comment, that Ted was "like Stepford," is an allusion to the 1975 film *The Stepford Wives,* a film that featured the "perfect wives," women who happily took on any domestic task to please their husbands. It was eerily appropriate considering that the Stepford wives were all robots!

\*   \*   \*

What was with the lighting in this episode? In several scenes, spotlighting appeared and disappeared without any apparent reason. Shadows flipped from one side of the mini-putt course to the other in just seconds; Buffy's nightstand is hidden in shadows one second, but brightly illuminated the next; Ted's "underbody" glitters in one shot but looks darkly dull in both the previous and following views. The lighting fluctuation might also have had something to do with the amount of squinting done by Sarah Michelle Gellar and Anthony Stewart Head in this episode.

\*   \*   \*

**ANSWERS**

1. D

2. A, B, and D

3. D

4. A

5. B

**What egg could feel safe with these parents? For that matter, which of these faux parents could feel safe with those eggs?!**

EPISODE:
# "Bad Eggs"

A

n exercise in "faux parenting" turns distinctly unsnuggly when Buffy's egg-baby ditches her for a slimy purple prehistoric parasite with an agenda all its own. Not only are the usual victims, her classmates, up to their ears—or necks—in trouble, but so are Buffy's mother, her sex ed teacher, and even her Watcher!

the short version

## A Tisket, a Tasket, a Faux-Baby Basket

the longer look

Not every student enrolled in a teen-parenting class is as blasé as egg-juggling Xander. Most develop a very real affection for their eggs—or faux-babies. Some, about one in two hundred, will actually continue to keep their make-believe babies long after the typical fourteen-day course has ended. An even rarer few, one in fifteen hundred, become obsessed with their little bundle of joy. A crack, a fall, or—horror of horrors!—the complete destruction of their precious package sinks them into a state of depression so deep that child psychologist Lauren Houghton of Toronto's Hospital for Sick Children likened it to "grief as real as some adults would feel at the loss of an actual child."

When Katie Powell, a twelve-year-old from eastern Florida, was given her egg as part of a voluntary sex ed course, she delighted in the opportunity to display her maternal instincts. Without any nudging from teacher or parents, Katie set her alarm for a six-week-old infant's four-hour schedule and

175

1. **Which actor's body makeup takes more than an hour to apply?**

   A. David Boreanaz
   B. Anthony Stewart Head
   C. Nicholas Brendon
   D. Armin Shimerman

2. **Which classic SF film also featured nasty things attaching themselves to human beings?**

   A. *Alien*
   B. *Invasion of the Body Snatchers*
   C. *Cocoon*
   D. *Contact*

3. **Which of the following actors *hasn't* portrayed a student in *Buffy the Vampire Slayer*?**

   A. Alexandra Johnes
   B. Musetta Vander
   C. Elizabeth Anne Allen
   D. Ryan James Bittle

4. **When was the original film version of *The Blob* released?**

   A. 1948
   B. 1958
   C. 1968
   D. 1988

---

## Who Was That?

**EPISODE PRODUCTION NUMBER: 5V12**
**ORIGINAL AIR DATE: JANUARY 12, 1998**
**WRITTEN BY: MARTI NOXON**
**DIRECTED BY: DAVID GREENWALT**

### CAST

| | |
|---|---|
| Buffy Summers | Sarah Michelle Gellar |
| Xander Harris | Nicholas Brendon |
| Willow Rosenberg | Alyson Hannigan |
| Cordelia Chase | Charisma Carpenter |
| Rupert Giles | Anthony Stewart Head |
| Angel | David Boreanaz |

### GUEST CAST

| | |
|---|---|
| Mrs. Joyce Summers | Kristine Sutherland |
| Jonathan | Danny Strong |
| Mr. Whitmore | Rick Zeiff |
| Tector Gorch | James Parks |
| Lyle Gorch | Jeremy Ratchford |

---

quickly adapted to the nap-when-you-can habits required of a real parent. She "power napped" through lunch, the morning recess, and just after supper. If anything, she was *too* good. Her teacher, after checking her parenting journal, was forced to gently suggest that no child needed to be changed *twenty* times a day! (We wonder if Xander ever changed his egg-baby—or did he see its little diaper as a convenient napkin?)

Katie's parents, somewhat confused by, but oddly proud of, their suddenly responsible daughter, happily obliged the girl's increasingly unusual schedule—even baby-sat while Katie took a "half hour off" to wash her hair. Her older brother, Calvin, was the only one who seemed to think Katie needed to "get a life away from that egg"! None of them were prepared for Katie's sudden plunge into despondency when, three weeks after the end of the faux-parenting experiment, her egg, kept raw to promote careful handling from the students, began to develop a distinct . . . odor.

Only after Katie's mother missed an entire bottle of bleach from the laundry, and discovered it secreted under her daughter's bedful of stuffed iguanas and frogs, did they begin to believe something was slightly "wiggins." Katie, in a vain attempt to take care of her egg's personal hygiene issues, had been soaking it in a bowl of Javex between rockings and "feedings." Her response to "Get a fresh egg, sweetie" was panicked tantrums and frantic attempts to curl her slender frame around her "Ovetta." Willow's instinctive egg-hugging on the library steps wasn't as overt, but, then again, she only had her egg for two days. What might Willow have been like after two weeks?

Dr. Mitchell Warren spent weeks not only weaning Katie from her egg, but explaining to her parents and teachers exactly how a

**5.** Whose dog developed a reputation for being difficult to "potty-train" while sharing a trailer with its owner on the *Buffy the Vampire Slayer* lot?

A. Sarah Michelle Gellar
B. Alyson Hannigan
C. Charisma Carpenter
D. Nicholas Brendon

## Everything I Ever Needed to Know, I Learned from *Buffy*

† Closets are erotic zones.

† Basements—especially those with suspiciously nonfunctional light switches and large tunnels in the walls—aren't happy places.

† Sunnydale's sex ed classes give new meaning to the phrase "A little knowledge is a dangerous thing"!

† Never turn your back on a librarian with a loaded drawer.

† Never answer rhetorical questions during sex ed.

† Sex in a Miata should be attempted on flat surfaces only.

† Purple stuff in a shell is *not* an approved after-school snack.

**ANSWERS**

1. **A**

2. **A**

3. **B**

4. **B**

5. **A**

previously well-adjusted young girl could possibly revert to the behavior of a two-year-old about to lose her "blankie": "Emotional maturity has nothing to do with physical age, though there are perfectly sound psychological reasons why twelve-year-olds shouldn't have children—even faux children. The whole point of the exercise is for the faux parent to act as if the egg were real. At twelve, Katie still had a child's ability to put herself deeply inside her own imaginings. Oddly enough, the fact that her parents were so very devoted to their children actually worked *against* her! She saw herself stepping into their shoes—and they were pretty big shoes for a young girl."

Maybe Xander *was* following in his parents' footsteps when he boiled his egg?

After all, they don't even recognize his voice on the phone.

About 30 percent of school boards have now amended their guidelines on faux-parenting classes to exclude participants under the age of fourteen. Others, however, despite encountering experiences similar to Katie's, are introducing the faux-parenting course to even *younger* students, especially the ten- to twelve-year-old age groups. "It's a little pointless to put students through the course *after* they've started experimenting," comments Michigan educator Lyle Koviaris. "We had two pregnancies in our grade-six class last year. One girl had just barely turned eleven! Putting off the faux-parenting program is the emotional equivalent to wearing blinders. Most of the parents who object to it simply don't want to believe their ten-year-old has an interest in sex."

Madeline Cohen has no illusions about teen and preteen sexuality. A teacher for twenty-three years and an educator with Planned Parenthood for another sixteen, Madeline has counseled clients as young as *nine*, but, like Lauren Houghton, has serious reservations about the whole faux-parenting program. "We had a tragic case in New Jersey just this week past—and neither Ardiss nor Arlene David, twins just turned eleven, were even part of a structured parenting program. They'd received a pair of those virtual pets for Christmas. Like Katie, they were dedicated little caregivers, and almost before their parents realized there was a problem, it was too late."

Ardiss's virtual puppy, Precious, was the first "death." Her parents assured her they could reset the device, but instead of playing

178

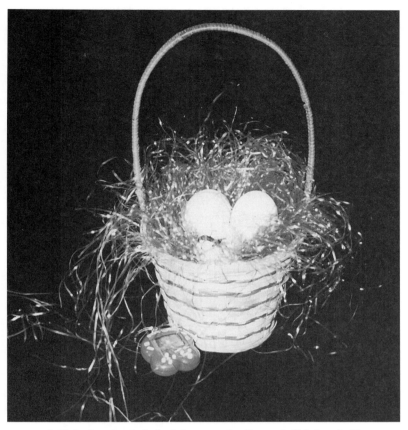

**A tisket, a tasket, betcha you don't want *this* basket!**

the game again, Ardiss held a highly ritualized funeral for her toy and buried it in the backyard. Dr. Warren would have seen that warning sign: "It's like parents who lose a child and then refuse to have any others, in the belief they'd somehow been disloyal to the first child. It's not unusual in cases of extreme attachment." He would have recognized the next sign as well. Within a week of Precious's death, Ardiss's teachers called home on three different occasions to remark on the girl's abrupt change of personality. Instead of the peppy girl who captained two sports teams and still managed to pull off an A average, their star pupil now skipped classes and flunked three exams in a row! No one connected the loss of her toy with her sudden depression. Dr. Warren continues, "In a sense, she was punishing herself for her failure. If she couldn't succeed as a 'parent,' well, she wouldn't allow herself to succeed—and receive the customary praise—in any other area of her life."

In retrospect, it was also easy to see that the only thing interrupting Ardiss's emotional fall were those rare moments when Arlene loaned her twin her own virtual pet. The girls lavished attention on the mechanical gizmo. Baby-sitting the critter became a mark of favor between them—a privilege to be earned.

If the Davids' story was a TV movie, the next scene would have been obvious. Like Buffy's GigaPet, Arlene's virtual kitty, Eleanor, met a violently messy end. Skittering off the edge of a condo balcony and tumbling seven stories to a paved parking area certainly voided all Eleanor's warranties, but unknown to the girls' parents, it also plunged the twins into a grief cycle that would end in a bathroom with every sort of tablet they could get their hands on. The double suicide, shocking under any circumstances, drew wide attention throughout medical and educational circles.

"We'd had cases of students becoming overly attached," notes Lauren Houghton. "It didn't seem any different than the separation anxiety of losing a pet—at least at first. Then we began noticing that these children, despite repeated assurances to the contrary, felt *guilt*—not just a natural loss. The experiment worked too well. We'd hoped to give them a sense of the responsibility parenthood brings. What we gave them was a burden they simply couldn't handle—on any level. The premise was, and remains, sound. We just have to be aware of the one in fifteen hundred children who might take the role-play that tad too far."

Not surprisingly, Houghton and the others have serious concerns about the latest prop in the faux-parenting scene—the Adopt-A-Baby Doll and its clones. Unlike eggs and virtual pets, the new dolls are anatomically correct replicas of real infants. They're heavy in all the right ways and places. They cry unless they're held just so. They cry if they aren't fed. They cry when their time-controlled bladders empty. They screech at the precise pitch and decibel level most likely to drive an adult, never mind an impressionable child, insane. Not unexpectedly, opinion on the lifelike creations is sharply divided. Dr. Warren cites the obvious concern. "If kids can become suicidally attached to a key chain, how would those same children react to this thing that not only actually gets warm and snuggly when it's happy, but condemns them loudly and vocally when it's laid down? I think reality-based education is too new—and untried—to be heralded as the cure-all for teen pregnancy."

Whatever concerns, valid or otherwise, are being tossed about in the staff rooms of high schools everywhere, Sunnydale probably remains unique in adding purple people-eaters to its list of educational criteria!

## Written on the Wall

It seems almost every program has its on-line fandom, and *Buffy the Vampire Slayer* is no exception. The staff acknowledged these loyal—and vocal—viewers about midway through "Bad Eggs." See that blackboard behind Willow? The words *Posting Board* written across it is a subtle nod of the head to the chatty folks at www.buffy-slayer.com, who spend hours doing some happy dissecting of their own—their theories about each and every episode!

\* \* \*

Oops! Lyle Gorch's "girlfriend" must have had a tough time beating her own high score. The pinball machine she was using, the same one Lyle bounced Buffy off of and vice versa, wasn't even on!

\* \* \*

Everyday Woman, Buffy's Mom's fave store, doesn't actually exist, but the mall shown in "Bad Eggs" most certainly does; it's the Sherman Oaks Galleria.

\* \* \*

Buffy's Eggbert wasn't just ugly, he defied the laws of physics. While Xander's little buddy had his growth arrested by boiling, Buffy's faux baby more than quadrupled its size in the time between its escape from the shell to its first scuttling trip under her bed just moments later!

\* \* \*

**Think they're thinking about STDs? Probably not,
but the network was!**

EPISODE:

# "Surprise" [Part 1]/ "Innocence" [Part 2]

the short version

"Surprise" (Part 1): Buffy's seventeenth birthday dawns with her prophetic dreams of Angel's death—and goes downhill from there! Not only does it appear that their old nemesis, Drusilla, is back to full strength—and insane as ever—but she and Spike have expanded their army to include the Judge. The bad guys don't even have the courtesy to let a poor, beleaguered Slayer celebrate with her nearest and dearest before they try to take over the world. Small wonder then that Buffy's first night with Angel turns out to be more than she expected.

"Innocence" (Part 2): After a single night together, Buffy and Angel discover just how persistent a Gypsy curse can be— and how devious. Having finally found true happiness, Angel's soul is once more taken from him, leaving the despicable demon calling itself Angelus in charge. After falling back in with his old partners, Angelus begins preying on Buffy's friends and family. Concentrating on her immediate problem—a big, blue demon with a plan to destroy humanity—just got harder.

## Your Intentions, How Honorable?

the longer look

*Sex. On network TV. In the new eight o'clock slot no less. With a virgin heroine. With a virgin heroine who'd have been jail bait in the state of California just hours ago. Yeah. Right.*
                                                                    —*Network Source*

# Who Was That?

EPISODE PRODUCTION NUMBERS: PART 1, "SURPRISE," 5V13
PART 2, "INNOCENCE," 5V14
ORIGINAL AIR DATES: PART 1, JANUARY 19, 1998
PART 2, JANUARY 20, 1998
WRITTEN BY: PART 1, MARTI NOXON
PART 2, JOSS WHEDON
DIRECTED BY: PART 1, MICHAEL LANGE
PART 2, JOSS WHEDON

## CAST

| | |
|---|---|
| Buffy Summers | Sarah Michelle Gellar |
| Xander Harris | Nicholas Brendon |
| Willow Rosenberg | Alyson Hannigan |
| Cordelia Chase | Charisma Carpenter |
| Rupert Giles | Anthony Stewart Head |

## GUEST CAST

| | |
|---|---|
| Angel | David Boreanaz |
| Oz | Seth Green |
| Mrs. Joyce Summers | Kristine Sutherland |
| Ms. Jenny Calendar | Robia La Morte |
| The Judge | Brian Thompson |
| Jenny's Uncle | Vincent Schiavelli |
| Spike | James Marsters |
| Drusilla | Juliet Landau |

**PART 1 ONLY**

Dalton                      Eric Saiet

**PART 2 ONLY**

Soldier                   Ryan Francis

Teacher                  James Lurie

Student                  Parry Shen

Woman                   Carla Madden

Despite its unlikely cast of characters, there's no doubt that *Buffy the Vampire Slayer*'s dramatic agenda is tightly wrapped up in the even more horrific events unfolding daily at a high school near you. Sex—having it, and not having it, and the point at which not having it turns into having it, were as inevitable a story line as any witch, vampire, or werewolf tale. Maneuvering the series's heroine into Angel's bed, and past the censor's desk, however, required a deft touch on both script and lens.

Drawing on Angel's established background as a "positively ancient" Irishman—despite his complete lack of accent, even a bad one—provided a few politically correct outs impossible in a strictly modern tale, outs tied to the exchange of those little bands of silver just before Angel's soul was once again evicted.

When Angel gives Buffy a ring, a match to his own, he tells her, "My people, before I was changed, exchanged this as a sign of devotion. It's a *claddagh* ring. The hands represent friendship. The crown represents loyalty. And the heart, well, you know. You wear it with the heart pointing towards you, it means you belong to somebody. Like this." Then, having made her aware of the symbolism, he asks her to put it on. Buffy must choose as the Hawaiian woman chooses behind which ear to tuck the traditional flower: placing it behind the left signifies she's heart-whole-and-fancy-free; placing it behind the right indicates she's committed elsewhere. However, the decision to wear her ring turned in or out is left completely to Buffy.

**QUESTIONS**

1. Whose real-life wife, Ingrid, gave him a real claddagh ring?

   A. Anthony Stewart Head
   B. James Marsters
   C. Ken Lerner
   D. David Boreanaz

2. In what country did Gypsies originate?

   A. Transylvania
   B. Bavaria
   C. Greece
   D. India

3. What is the Gypsy word for "vampire"?

   A. Mulo
   B. Gudo
   C. Fakir
   D. Creb

4. Which actor played a vampire on two different series?

   A. David Boreanaz
   B. Brian Thompson
   C. Mark Metcalf
   D. James Marsters

## Everything I Ever Needed to Know, I Learned from *Buffy*

† Catering for a vampire function is a real breeze—it's a much more limited menu than usual.

† If someone mentions the "slow boat to China" as a real travel option, check their teeth.

† All-night optometrists have their uses.

† Party crashing is dangerous to your health.

† "You don't call it a 'date' until the guy spends money." —Cordelia, on broom closets and dates

† Even demons need to "mall" now and then.

† The perfect gift for the Slayer with everything? A LAWS rocket.

Buffy chooses to slide it on with the heart facing in—signifying her consent to an exclusive relationship—at least according to the terms Angel outlined.

A short ditty that's been photocopied onto tons of high-quality fake vellum scrolls, and tucked inside as many velour boxes, suggests Angel wasn't in full-disclosure mode. It reads:

*Worn to the right, with heart facing outward
tells the world your heart has yet to be won.*

*Worn to the right, with heart facing inward
tells the world love may have captured your heart.
Worn to the left, with the heart inward, closest to you
shouts your love eternal and true.*

Then again, Angel is more than *two hundred years old*. Maybe he hasn't been back to Ireland since the advent of fake vellum, velour

Who knew accessories could play such an important role?

5. **Traditionally, what Gypsy practices warded off vampires?**

   A. Hanging garlic about the house
   B. Pouring boiling water over the grave
   C. Sewing an iron nail into your clothes
   D. Driving a steel needle into a corpse's heart

boxes, and other touristy additions to the story. For that matter, maybe he's not up on that other new-fangled tradition—engagement.

Two hundred years ago, across most of Europe, including the island of Ireland, a betrothal was as binding as any formal marriage service or contract. On the strength of a mutually acknowledged engagement, valuable lands, herds, and gold could be exchanged. The usual waiting period, if there was one at all, was often to allow the woman to reach childbearing age. Should the bride-to-be already have reached that physiological age, young as that might be, it wasn't unusual to have the bedding before the wedding—especially in areas where the religious authority was itinerant and might

**ANSWERS**

**1. D**

**2. D**

**3. A**

**4. B**

**5. A, B, C and D**

**What to give the Slayer who has everything for her birthday!**

not be available for several months. As long as all was in order before the arrival of the first child, there was little impropriety associated with these early "common-law" relationships.

Some areas even had formalized rituals meant to tide a couple over in the eyes of the community until they found a priest. One ceremony required only that the couple indicate their consent before two of their neighbors—the precursor to witnesses in modern marriage ceremonies—and exchange something of value. In Dulherry, Ireland, the couple needed only lay their hands on the town's altar and declare themselves married! No witnesses, no rings, nothing. It was understood that God himself was the witness, obviating the need for any other ritual. These informal arrangements were more the rule than the exception for those with little or no goods to argue over, and in not allowing Angel's origins to be romanticized into the realm of even landed gentry, the writers avoided entangling him in a prior lifestyle that would expect him to exchange more than promises and tokens with Buffy. Like the *claddagh* ring he gave to Buffy, silver instead of the more opulent gold, his expectations for the rituals establishing a binding relationship may have been much simpler.

Pushed to defend their romantic portrayal of what might otherwise be called the tacky deflowering of a junior in high school, the

The Judge is looking familiar? Not surprising, really. The makeup was decidedly lighter in his first appearance on *Buffy,* when he played Luke, the Master's Vessel in the series premiere, but his impressive presence, due only in part to his physical stature, remains unmistakable.

\* \* \*

Perhaps it was the simultaneous success of *Buffy the Vampire Slayer* and the newly released video version of *Toy Story,* which Whedon scripted, or maybe it was the switch from Monday to Tuesday night in the North American market. . . . Whatever the reason, "Surprise" was the first episode to feature promos—for the second half of the two-parter, "Innocence"—declaring our favorite show to be "Joss Whedon's *Buffy the Vampire Slayer.*"

\* \* \*

Even if you weren't busy trying to figure out how a vampire with no breath managed to steal a drag off his victim's cigarette through the side of her throat, or how a creature lacking such basics as a pulse or blood pressure works around those obstacles to physically satisfy an incredibly buff teenager, those transition scenes between "Surprise" and "Innocence" must have left you wondering what *else* Buffy and Angel did during their night of passion.

Somewhere along the line, Buffy managed to pop in an extra earring and paint her nails a brilliant metallic silver while she basked in the afterglow—then dissolve the nail polish again before attempting to sneak home! She painted her nails but didn't look for her missing lover?

Of course, Angel was obviously too busy to notice any distraction on his date's part. Somewhere between awakening naked, except for a pair of black undies, to the agony of having his soul stripped away, and collapsing in a downpour in a nearby alley, he found time to rummage through his closet, get completely dressed in clothes other than those he likely dropped by the bed the night before, color-coordinate a really nifty outfit, and neatly do up all his zippers, buttons, and laces! Not bad for a guy last seen screaming his head off . . .

And speaking of that screaming, how was it that Buffy, the ultrasensitive Slayer, never heard a thing? And, if Angel was screaming for Buffy, why did he stagger out into a rainstorm instead of just turning over under his comfy sheets? Not that the rain seemed to bother him too much, of course. Between one camera angle and the next, a matter of mere seconds, Angel managed to change from a water-sodden near-invalid to a completely dry supervillain!

* * *

If you happened to notice anything other than the flying heels during Buffy's fight scene in the movie theater, you undoubtedly noticed the dozens of posters promoting the upcoming animated film *Quest for Camelot*. No, there's no link between the film and any member of the *BTVS* cast, it's just a not-so-subtle attempt to induce viewers to watch yet another WB project!

* * *

"Oz has a van." *A* van? That's sort of like saying Willow has *a* backpack! Viewers might be able to convince themselves that Oz just liked to paint his van. After all, it was zebra-striped in one episode, plain vanilla in "Innocence," right? Right. But how's a viewer to explain the fact that the *steering wheel changed sides*?

* * *

Oops. Hey, remember Xander's frantic CPR scene with Buffy in "Prophecy Girl"? The one that begins with Angel's angst-filled admission that he has "no breath" and therefore can't save her? And remember how Angel dove into the gas-filled boiler room to rescue Giles and the others?

> The action was made possible by the fact that he doesn't breathe, right? Guess Buffy and her Slayerettes would have been awfully surprised to see Angel sucking his victim's neck with enough enthusiasm to steal a drag as well as a pint or two! Vampires must give killer hickeys.
>
> * * *

writers have left enough mystery and vaguely remembered traditions hovering about Angel for them to claim that under Irish tradition, Buffy and Angel were soundly married before sliding between Angel's richly draped sheets! Now, what questions that raises!

Now that Angel's soul has been tossed out, is Buffy a widow? Or, knowing that Angel's soul was conjured back from some odd netherworld plane by the original curse, is she still "married" to some disembodied spirit, the Angel she knows? And what exactly is the statute of limitations for determining legal death for a vampire? How long is a girl supposed to wait? Seven years, the human equivalent, seems stingy for a creature already working on its third century of "life." And what does a woman wear while in mourning for someone who died two hundred–plus years before she was even *born*?

For that matter, why is Angelus, supposedly obsessed with bloody dreams of vengeance, still wearing *his* ring in later episodes? Even when he hands Drusilla her gory Valentine's Day heart, the silver band gleams dully on his hand!

And perhaps the biggest question of all? Suppose Angelus is once more subsumed by a magically restored Angel, just where does that leave the tragic couple? Unlike other couples who can just kiss and make up, this pair have the little matter of mutually attempted murder to resolve!

Could Emily Post unsnarl the confused issues surrounding this couple?

**Seth Green with more—and less!—hair than seen in "Phases."**

EPISODE:

"Phases"

the short version

ust when it seems Willow's love life is finally looking up and the vampires are cooperating by hanging out elsewhere for a few nights, a new, more furry, threat invades beleaguered Sunnydale and starts depopulating Lover's Lane. So, instead of hanging with a cool band guy, and moving up from the bottom rung of Sunnydale High's social ladder, Willow, along with Buffy, Xander, Cordelia, and an "intrigued" Rupert, race to find a werewolf who's already on a professional hunter's hit list.

## What's a Little Howling Between Friends?

the longer look

*I—I am quite intrigued. Werewolves! It's one of the classics! Yes, I'm sure my books and I are in for a fascinating afternoon!*
*—Rupert Giles*

Rupert Giles isn't the first person to be fascinated by tales of shape-shifting humans who, either at will or at regularly scheduled phases of the moon, change themselves into ferocious, fearless lupine hunters. These "classic" monsters, featured in literature as far back as the *Epic of Gilgamesh* circa 2,000 B.C., have certainly filled tons of the books Giles is so enamored of. Unfortunately, from the werewolf hunter's point of view, the books are all contradictory!

## Who Was That?

**EPISODE PRODUCTION NUMBER: 5V15**

**ORIGINAL AIR DATE: JANUARY 27, 1998**

**WRITTEN BY: ROB DES HOTEL AND DEAN BATALI**

**DIRECTED BY: BRUCE SETH GREEN**

### CAST

| | |
|---|---|
| Buffy Summers | Sarah Michelle Gellar |
| Xander Harris | Nicholas Brendon |
| Willow Rosenberg | Alyson Hannigan |
| Cordelia Chase | Charisma Carpenter |
| Rupert Giles | Anthony Stewart Head |
| Angelus (Angel) | David Boreanaz |

### GUEST CAST

| | |
|---|---|
| Oz | Seth Green |
| Cain | Jack Conley |
| Gym Teacher | Camila Griggs |
| Larry | Larry Bagby III |
| Theresa Klusmeyer | Meghan Perry |
| Werewolf | Keith Campbell |

For starters, they can't even agree on how you *become* a werewolf! Judging from Oz's conversations with his relatives, lycanthropy is either hereditary or contagious—or both. Oz's uncle was a werewolf, and so was the uncle's son, Oz's cousin, Jordy—the same Jordy who decided to cut his grown-up teeth on Oz. Should Giles decide to establish whether it was werewolf germs or genetics that

194

causes Oz's furry periods (or if Willow investigates, for that matter, as she has a vested interest in the answer), the first thing he'll discover is that lycanthropy has dozens of traditional sources.

Not surprisingly, contact with real wolves ranks high on the list of possible sources of contamination. Eating wolf parts, especially the brain or footpads, seemed a guaranteed prescription for furriness. Wearing clothing made from lupine pelts, especially the wolf-skin belt mentioned in several European accounts, was explained as a way that unsuspecting vegetarians could contract the dreaded disease. Even those with absolutely *no* contact with the creatures might well have been "poisoned" by ill-wishers who'd collected water from the paw print of a wolf, or even better, from puddles a

---

## Everything I Ever Needed to Know, I Learned from *Buffy*

† Werewolves have no respect for convertibles.

† Grabbing a Slayer's ass is detrimental to your health.

† Bringing a flashlight to Lover's Lane might
be construed as overaccessorizing.

† Waking up alone and naked in the woods
definitely qualifies as a Bad Thing.

† When a guy fixes your clothing tags, it's the real thing.

† Hanging a Slayer upside down inside a net is
a sure way to piss her off.

† The boys' locker room probably isn't the best place
to discuss "alternative" lifestyles.

† Secrets discovered by snooping around car windows
should remain sacrosanct.

† A boyfriend who keeps manacles in his kitchen—
and has never seen you by the light of a romantic full moon—
probably bears closer investigation.

## QUESTIONS

1. Who was born February 8, 1974?

   A. Seth Green
   B. James Marsters
   C. Robia La Morte
   D. David Boreanaz

2. Which of the following films *isn't* about were-wolves?

   A. *Silver Bullet*
   B. *Howl*
   C. *The Howling*
   D. *Bad Moon Rising*

3. Which outside company is responsible for the special effects makeup on *Buffy the Vampire Slayer*?

   A. Industrial Light and Magic
   B. Optic Nerve Studios
   C. The Creature Hut
   D. Area 51

4. Which *Buffy the Vampire Slayer* regular had pictures of his/her birth used in a natural childbirth advertisement?

   A. David Boreanaz
   B. Sarah Michelle Gellar
   C. Seth Green
   D. Alyson Hannigan

Oz is following in the classic footsteps of Lon Chaney, Jr., who's pictured here in *The Wolfman*.

werewolf may have lapped from. Of course, being bitten by a were-wolf is almost universally agreed to work pretty well, too.

During the height of the lycanthropy trials in Europe, all things lupine, even completely unconnected and inanimate objects, were considered suspect. Planting wolfsbane in your front yard, which might seem the act of someone trying to *avoid* sprouting hair in polite company, took on ominous overtones in thirteenth-century Germany. A badly translated letter from a distant bishopric resulted in a widespread belief that wolfsbane grew most heavily along woodland trails frequented by werewolves—and on the properties of werewolves hiding among humans! Outside Klein-

Krams, a very localized bit of folklore held that growing wolfsbane wasn't a sign of lycanthropy but a direct cause that could turn perfectly normal human beings into ravening beasts.

Other communities accepted even more tenuous causes. Tasting human flesh, even inadvertently, caused instant affliction. Being born on Christmas Eve, while not guaranteed to result in sprouting hair and the need for a nose job, served as a warning to the child's parents that *this one* needed watching, and extra protection from all the other hazards floating around. Associating with known criminals, handling frogs, engaging in premarital sex, homosexual sex, sex in general, for that matter, or desecrating a church were all perilous activities. So were sleeping under a new moon, crossing water counterclockwise in a boat (Like, why would anyone do that, anyway?), eating bats (Again, like, why?), associating with a witch, or, of course, sleeping with a witch (Wanna bet Willow eyes that one closely?).

Naturally, sleeping with a wolf or a bona fide werewolf wasn't a good plan, either, which brings up the next set of contradictions brought together under the werewolf mythos. In order to avoid touching, eating, or sleeping with a werewolf, believers in the creatures had to find some surefire way of determining just who was, or wasn't, a werewolf. Willow would do well to brush up on these herself.

Perhaps if she'd called out, "Oz, Oz, Oz!" he'd have turned back into his adorable self as Balkan legends claim—assuming Oz is his true birth name. If his parents weren't really that cool, however, there were still ways to root out the truth. According to some Polish traditions, werewolves' aversion to metal isn't restricted to silver bullets. Passing a metal object over a werewolf, or compelling the werewolf to run under something metal, negated the effect of wolf belts and wolfskins and left the were-creature standing in its human form. Perhaps because of their silver backing, mirrors would prove equally useful in separating the boys from the werewolves. Unlike a vampire, who usually can't be seen in a mirror, a werewolf stands literally naked before it as the appearance of its animal self is stripped away.

And how do you recognize a werewolf in its human form? Well,

5. Which film *didn't* feature both a vampire and a werewolf?
   A. *The Return of the Vampire*
   B. *Abbott and Costello Meet Frankenstein*
   C. *Howling VI: The Freaks*
   D. *Wolf*

ANSWERS

1. A

2. B

3. B

4. C

5. D

the guy who looks like the boy next door can often be revealed by his hairy palms, long thumbnails, extra long ring fingers, or a tendency to sleep with his mouth open. Of course, Cordelia might say that describes most high-school juniors!

If medieval werewolf hunters were so interested in determining the human identity of their targets, it may have been because they recognized two types of werewolf: one, a victim and the other, a voluntary shape-shifter who delighted in ravaging his community. For those unintentional practitioners such as Oz, an elaborate series of "cures," laid out by nearly every culture, awaited. For the deliberate werewolf who delighted in his predations, however, some serious and deadly countermeasures were necessary.

The silver bullet, the long-established weapon of werewolf hunters such as Cain, Sunnydale's own werewolf hunter, figures in at least four different folk traditions. Most of the lore, the Buffyverse included, equates the silver bullet to the vampire hunter's stake—an instant, dramatic, and guaranteed way to off wandering lycanthropes. A Romanian hunter, however, would find his supply of bullets much more restricted than Cain's. According to the Romanian stories, only silver that came to the hunter through inheritance could be forged into effective bullets. Regular silver wouldn't be any more useful than sticks and stones. In Klein-Krams, Germany, where an infamous werewolf reportedly killed off dozens of people, the bullet that finally stopped the rampage was not only made of inherited silver, but sacred silver, in the sense that the bullet was a religious medal in its former incarnation. Perhaps the success of that hunt was the source of Germany's widespread belief that only melted-down holy objects would work. A letter written in 1437 to a Father Niceé tells of a mob raiding a church for enough silver to prepare "forty bullets of the sort to destroy the wolf." However, a fourth set of legends, apparently Baltic in origin, never claimed that silver itself could kill a werewolf. Instead, in these and related Scandinavian tales, silver, which could as easily be a silver knife as a silver bullet, caused "wounds which never closed." The werewolf actually died of infection, blood loss, or the lethal actions perpetrated by a mob who could catch the injured creature more easily.

In addition to silver bullets, werewolf hunters had other tricks up their sleeves. Running the creature through with any number of "magical" wooden rods made from ash, oak, or alder would kill it. So would burning it, or its human form, at the stake. Confining a werewolf inside a church until it changed form worked most of the time, if the Prussian chronicles are to be believed. Drowning, the preferred method in Scandinavia, also found favor with Siberians and Ukrainians. Austrians developed highly ritualized ceremonies featuring drawing and quartering, beheading, burning, and a short period of playing with the creature's entrails with hot irons.

Considering the lengthy lists of atrocities attributed to these classic monsters, it's almost surprising that any cures were ever attempted! At the height of the medieval werewolf scare, more than eleven hundred deaths were credited to them in a single year in Germany alone. Still, unlike vampires, usually portrayed as irredeemable, werewolves received the benefit of the doubt in many European communities, and rituals of sorts were devised to control or cure the lycanthrope's condition.

Simply catching werewolves was tough, so most schemes to cure them actually began with lengthy lists of capture techniques. A pity Buffy hadn't read the list before chasing down Oz! Most monster tales feature quasi-religious overtones, and catching werewolves often involved church vigils for the prospective hunters, blessings for their weapons, and holy medals by the dozen. It's not too surprising that prayer became a werewolf-hunting tool as well. In southern Bavaria, it was widely believed that a circle of chanting monks could contain a lycanthrope in either its human or lupine form. In the northern Bavarian regions, the preferred method of catching werewolves was to trick them into positions where they were surrounded by running water. One village lured their beast onto a raft, then set the raft afloat until morning, when the human form reappeared. Braevestrau residents dammed a small brook, set out a sacrificial lamb, and rerouted the water once again, catching their local lycanthrope without ever getting within claw range. Rings of rose petals, holy wafers, garlic buds, or salt were common means of fencing in werewolves, as were thorn hedges, a braided circle of freshly cut barley or rye grasses, or a werewolf's worst

# Written on the Wall

The Bronze hosted dozens of terrific real-world musicians during the first season and a half of *Buffy the Vampire Slayer*. This episode's distinctive tunes were provided by Lotion.

*   *   *

Look up a definition of *clean-cut* in any dictionary, and a picture of Willow's gamine face will stare back at you. But well-scrubbed as that face may be, does that explain how she could tumble in the dirt while escaping a werewolf, run straight to the rest of the gang at the library, and arrive with absolutely pristine clothes? What happened to all the stains that are obviously visible after she scrambles to her feet and runs away?

*   *   *

This episode, with all its little references to previous programs, was an absolute delight for those faithful viewers seeking another excuse to exercise their memories and observation skills. "I, Robot—You, Jane," which featured Willow's less-than-successful romance with a cyberdemon, inspired Xander's "Robby the Robot's love slave" comments, while "Teacher's Pet" provided context for the otherwise senseless remarks about Xander's losing his head. Locker stickers for bands like Velvet Chain spark memories of the great tunes performed in "Never Kill a Boy on the First Date." Even the opening scene of "Phases," in which Oz stares at a trophy that really does stare right back, is an allusion to a previous episode of *Buffy*, "The Witch." While hardly essential to the overall story line of "Phases," these little perks never fail to bring an extra grin to fans' faces.

*   *   *

enemy, fire. One odd tale suggests that trapping a werewolf inside a cemetery until daylight was also pretty effective, but doesn't suggest just how you'd force the creature to stay there.

Of course, just catching the werewolf wasn't the real point (except perhaps in southern France, where reports still survive of a generous reward being offered by a traveling entertainment troupe to anyone who provided a werewolf for their sideshow act). Once caught, a "tiger by the tail" situation quickly developed, forcing the hunters to either cure their victim immediately, or for the sake of the neighborhood, kill it. Unfortunately for the werewolf, the cures often seemed more brutal than the killings!

Beating was very popular. Bavarians beat their werewolves with alder switches. Germans slashed and battered theirs with raspberry canes. Londoners were more forceful and bashed their were-critters with oak cudgels. The Latvian custom of beating lycanthropes with braided thread may have seemed relatively gentle—until you realize that the thread was silver and reputedly left the victim suffering from scores of deep incisions that bled profusely!

If beating didn't work, there were still other options, though few seemed risk-free. Burial in consecrated ground for a day and a night was said to be effective—if the victim didn't simply smother. Dunking in holy water had the obvious disadvantage of drowning the patient. Victims barred inside churches for the requisite three days actually died of dehydration because hunters refused to bring them water. Of all the cures, however, Prague's was the most drastic. Its werewolves, sandwiched between huge metal grills, were suspended over banked coals while a priest prayed over them for a full day and night. Needless to say, even the survivors suffered gross disfigurement. Compared to that cure, a silver bullet to the heart or the brain seemed downright humane.

Small wonder Oz opted to manacle himself to some sturdy furniture for a few days a month.

**Broom closet, anyone?**

# "Bewitched, Bothered, and Bewildered"

the short version

When Xander finds himself the object of ridicule and pity after Cordelia dumps him in an incredibly public way at The Bronze's Valentine's dance, he turns to his friend and classmate—not to mention neighborhood witch—Amy for a love potion. Unfortunately, Amy's spell goes awry, and Xander must flee a mob of obsessed female fans, including an ax-wielding Willow, an infatuated vampiress, and Buffy's mom! Even more unfortunately, Cordelia, the object of Xander's spell, is the one woman in all of Sunnydale who still won't have anything to do with him.

## Charmed to Meet You

the longer look

**Amy:** *Intent has to be pure with love spells.*
**Xander:** *Right. I intend revenge. Pure as the driven snow.*

Love may be a many splendored thing, but as Xander discovered, love spells have a dark side. Even modern Wiccans and their spiritual kin remain divided on whether or not such spells violate the craft's only real rule, "An it harm none, do what thou will." Free will, the exercise of choice, and respect for individuals are all powerful tenets of the neopagan movement,

203

# Who Was That?

EPISODE PRODUCTION NUMBER: 5V16
ORIGINAL AIR DATE: FEBRUARY 9, 1998
WRITTEN BY: MARTI NOXON
DIRECTED BY: JAMES A. CONTNER

## CAST

| | |
|---|---|
| Buffy Summers | Sarah Michelle Gellar |
| Xander Harris | Nicholas Brendon |
| Willow Rosenberg | Alyson Hannigan |
| Cordelia Chase | Charisma Carpenter |
| Rupert Giles | Anthony Stewart Head |
| Angel | David Boreanaz |

## GUEST CAST

| | |
|---|---|
| Oz | Seth Green |
| Mrs. Joyce Summers | Kristine Sutherland |
| Ms. Jenny Calendar | Robia La Morte |
| Amy | Elizabeth Anne Allen |
| Harmony | Mercedes McNab |
| Devon | Jason Hall |
| Kate | Jennie Chester |
| Cordette | Kristen Winnicki |
| Jock | Scott Hamm |
| Frenzied Girl | Tamara Braun |
| Spike | James Marsters |
| Drusilla | Juliet Landau |
| Miss Beakman | Lorna Scott |

especially those traditions that also embrace the womanist and environmental ethos. Yet, despite the apparently obvious violation of the subject's free will, love spells, charms, and philters figure prominently in the magical traditions of nearly every region. Some themes and rites, such as the one Amy performed—or misperformed, depending on your point of view—appear universal, but a few remain standouts for their bizarre procedures or ingredients. So, if your intention is pure, maybe you'll find something in this mini magic book.

From Tibet comes the Ritual of the Red Thread, which, frankly, leaves one wondering just how unwilling to accept a lover the subject would have to be! In this combination of incantation and ritual, a fine silk thread (red, of course) is wound around the intended lover, taking the "measure" of the man's or woman's figure and, metaphysically speaking, of the soul. The physical binding of the thread requires some 112 knots to be tied. The first, not surprisingly, is located above the heart, but the position of some of the others leaves one scratching one's head. What could possibly be *less* romantic than the left nostril? Precious little other than foot corns, yet that knot above the nostril seems key to determining the intended's fitness. Oh, well, beauty is in the eye of the beholder.

Once the complicated tangle is marked and removed, a process

---

## Everything I Ever Needed to Know, I Learned from *Buffy*

✝ If it's not a date until the guy spends money, then it's not a Valentine present until the girl gets cuddly.

✝ Sitting naked in a chem lab is probably *not* the way to get dates.

✝ Two-timing a Vampire Slayer—or her mother— is dangerous to your health.

✝ The two concepts "tongues" and "best friend's mother" shouldn't appear in the same thought.

1. Which *Buffy the Vampire Slayer* regular grew up in Las Vegas, Nevada?

   A. Sarah Michelle Gellar
   B. Kristine Sutherland
   C. Alyson Hannigan
   D. Charisma Carpenter

2. Which of the following *isn't* a god of love?

   A. Aphrodite
   B. Cupid
   C. Venus
   D. Hel

3. Which *Buffy the Vampire Slayer* cast member got married after joining the show?

   A. Anthony Stewart Head
   B. David Boreanaz
   C. Alyson Hannigan
   D. Seth Green

4. Who is Juliet Landau's mother?

   A. Barbara Bain
   B. Catherine Deneuve
   C. Audrey Hepburn
   D. Judy Garland

that can take up to four hours, the hair-thin silk is coiled and curled into a thicker cord and twisted around the practitioner's wrist, and the rest of the ritual is played out. Over the course of the next three lunar cycles, the spell caster alternates with snow and steam baths, fasts and gorges. (Doesn't a cold shower seem simpler?) The "victim," who, for some reason, makes no effort to extricate himself from the spell caster's enchantment, is even invited to several of the principal events! The spell caster's efforts are judged successful when the subject not only accepts one of these invitations, but moves in with the inviter! At that point, the band is cut free and returned in pieces to the new lover as they live happily ever after.

Somehow, it's hard to picture Cordy patiently waiting for Xander to encase her in red silk—well, maybe, if it was Armani—much less endure his attempts at cooking or, horror of horrors, a friendly roll in the snow! No, Xander's ploys would have to be much more sophisticated than that!

The Old World has no lock on love spells. Even a young country such as the United States has regional magical traditions, some of them quite charming, and some of them sneaky enough to satisfy Xander's needs without leaving him half-naked in the middle of a chemistry lab!

"To catch your love, be quiet twice. Once to whisper your name in their ear—but don't let them hear! Again, on the night of the

**Think she got it back again?**

## Written on the Wall

**Though Willow is undoubtedly the cutest groupie ever to grace The Bronze, and Dingoes Ate My Baby is perhaps the gnarliest name for a Bronze band, it'd be a downright shame not to mention Four Star Mary. They're the *real* band backing Oz during the appearances that set Willow to chair dancing!**

\* \* \*

**Score one in the irony column. With this episode being the first after the audience learned of Oz's alter ego, the were-wolf, it seems highly appropriate that he be the one to discover a naked Slayer in a strange basement. After all, he'd undoubtedly found himself in the same situation at least three nights a month!**

\* \* \*

**5. Who handles special visual effects, such as "magic sparkling things that swirl across the room," for *Buffy the Vampire Slayer*?**

A. Industrial Light and Magic
B. Optic Nerve Studios
C. The Creature Hut
D. Area 51

hidden moon, to call them to you on the dark breeze." Even Xander couldn't screw up that bit of folk magic from Appalachia! Could he?

The Castaway Charm of the Papua New Guineans is another spell that falls into the sneaky category. Starting with some item of the beloved's, preferably something intensely personal such as hair or blood, the caster skulks off into the most convenient patch of dense shrubbery available, digs a hole, buries the hair or whatever, and then dances skyclad—naked, to the nonpagan community— around the hole. After praying, singing, and urinating over the tiny depression, the caster replaces the soil and sleeps above the spot for the next seven nights. Still completely invisible to the object of his affection, the lovesick spell weaver's next action is to dig up the dirt once more and skulk back through the bushes to his loved one's home, where he proceeds to scatter the urine-soaked soil over her front steps!

If she doesn't clue in to his little bit of prestidigitation at that point, well, he can sneak off again, confident that about seven days later, he'll have a brand-new lover, with smelly feet.

**ANSWERS**

**1. D**

**2. D**

**3. B**

**4. A**

**5. D**

**Wonder if you could still find mutilated Barbies in Amy's attic?**

However, if she does notice the odd-smelling mess tossed across her threshold, and consciously rejects him, he'll spend the next thirteen lunar cycles being repeatedly, and irresistibly, drawn back to his little hole in the woods.

Somehow, traditions like that make the whole club scene seem rather tame.

For colorful antics, however, the peasant rituals of Iraq have few comparisons. When a member of the Balahani clan decides he's found the one for him, he skips the heart-shaped boxes of candy, the flowers, the jewelry that costs him more goats than he can afford, and the time-consuming business of actually courting! No, he speaks to the clan's adviser, who turns him over to the spiritual leader, or *misha,* which in some other cultures would be called the tribe's witch doctor. For a sum equal to about half the number of goats he might have had to dish out, the spiritual leader takes on the whole "dating" process for him! On the first night, the witch doctor parks himself in front of the girl's home and shouts out slogans designed to impress her, things like "His herds will overrun you!" and "Your womb will never be empty!" If that fails to get her instant agreement, he'll spend the next day back in front of her house, describing what her life will be like should she not accept her absentee lover: "Your face will wrinkle and be covered in blotches"; "Hair will grow from your chin." Still not interested? "Diseases of the genitals will afflict you"; "A thousand men will take you as you scream."

While not particularly pleasant, such shouting sessions don't really qualify as magical rituals—that's the third day's agenda.

Armed with one of the goats, a big knife, a dozen multicolored flags, a set of cymbals, and some incense that most resembles dried dung (probably from the goat), the *misha* gets serious. Beginning with a sunrise ceremony during which he burns the girl in effigy, he continues through the day until he works himself up to slaughtering the goat, who has been standing in the sun all day. As the sun sets, he flicks the blood over the poor woman's home, curses her father and brothers, casts aspersions on any female relatives in the neighborhood, and heads off home, firm in his belief that unless she accepts her suitor with open arms (this is a love spell, remember), she'll break out in genital herpes or worse by daybreak. Few women make it to morning without a betrothal being announced. Of course, that may have more to do with finance than magical ability. According to this same tradition, if the ritual isn't successful, the young man doesn't have to pay. Instead, the *misha* bills the girl's parents!

Seem a bit sexist? Well, it is! Still, though women have the reputation for working their wiles on unsuspecting men, the magical history that still survives strongly indicates it's the *men* who are most likely to seek a little supernatural help in the dating game. Guess Xander isn't completely alone inside his little circle in the chemistry lab.

**Will we ever see these happier days again?**

# "*Passion*"

Just as Jenny Calendar seems poised to restore Angel's soul with her own blend of cyber-intelligence and magic, Angelus, the demon residing in Angel's body, starts delivering on his promise to kill off Buffy's friends and family. Her mother, Willow, and even her not-nearly-best friend Cordelia quickly find themselves regretting the hospitality that now allows the "reformed" vampire such easy access to their homes. A desperate scramble to find new metaphysical locks may be too late.

the short version

## I Fall to Pieces

With the first throbbing notes of *Buffy the Vampire Slayer*'s theme, alternative-music fans *knew* they were in for some of the hip-hoppin'est tunes to pump up a television series in years. Nerf Herder's raunchy beat, given a seemingly endless number of variations as it wove its way through hours of action sequences, quickly struck the right tone with everyone from the "dubba-dubba-dubba-u-b" execs to seemingly all of even *Buffy*'s demographically divergent audience. While everyone might recognize the essential elements of *Buffy*dom's music—well, with the notable exception of Xander's "music of pain"

the longer look

211

| EPISODE | ARTIST | SONG, ALBUM |
|---|---|---|
| "The Witch" | 2 Unlimited | "Twilight Zone," *Get Ready* |
| "Teacher's Pet" | Superfine | "Already Met You," *Stoner Love* |
| | | "Stoner Love," *Stoner Love* |
| "Never Kill a Boy on the First Date" | Three Day Wheely | "Rotten Apple," *Rubber Halo* |
| | Kim Richey | "Let the Sun Fall Down," *Kim Richey* |
| | Rubber | "Junky Girl," *Rubber* |
| | Velvet Chain | "Strong," *Groovy Side* |
| | | "Treason," *Groovy Side* |
| "The Pack" | Far | "Job's Eyes," *Tin Cans with Strings to You* |
| "Angel" | Sophie Zelmani | "I'll Remember You," *Sophie Zelmani* |
| "Prophecy Girl" | Jonatha Brooke & The Story | "Inconsolable," *Plumb* |
| | Patsy Cline | "I Fall to Pieces," *The Patsy Cline Story* |
| "When She Was Bad" | Cibo Matto | "Spoon," *Super Relax* |
| | | "Sugar Water," *Viva! La Woman* |
| | Alison Krauss & Union Station | "It Doesn't Matter," *So Long So Wrong* |
| "School Hard" | Nickel | "1000 Nights," *Stupid Thing* |
| | | "Stupid Thing," *Stupid Thing* |
| "Inca Mummy Girl" | Four Star Mary | "Shadows," *Four Star Mary* |
| | | "Fate," *Four Star Mary* |
| "Reptile Boy" | Act of Faith | "Bring Me On," *Delta Zeta Kappa* |
| | Louie Says | "She," *Gravity, Suffering, Love and Fate* |
| "Halloween" | Epperley | "Shy," *Epperley* |

| | Treble Charger | "How She Died," *Maybe It's Me* |
|---|---|---|
| "Lie to Me" | Creaming Jesus | "Reptile," *Gothic Rocki* |
| | The Sisters of Mercy | "Never Land," *Floodland* |
| | Willoughby | "Lois, on the Brink," *Be Better Soon* |
| "Surprise" | Rasputina | "Transylvanian Concubine," *Thanks for the Ether* |
| "Phases" | Lotion | "Blind for Now," *Nobody's Cool* |
| "Bewitched, Bothered, and Bewildered" | The Average White Band | "Got the Love," *The Average White Band* |
| | Four Star Mary | "Pain," *Four Star Mary* |
| | Naked | "Drift Away," *Naked* |
| "Passion" | Morcheeba | "Never an Easy Way," *Who Can You Trust?* |
| "I Only Have Eyes for You" | The Flamingos | "I Only Have Eyes for You," *The Best of The Flamingos* |
| | Splendid | "Charge," Live performances only |
| "Go Fish" | Naked | "Mann's Chinese," *Naked* |
| | Nero's Rome | "If You'd Listen," *Togetherly* |
| "Becoming" | Sarah McLachlan | "Full of Grace," *Surfacing* |

collection—the low grind, the quirky lyrics, and the grunge-cum-something-even-cooler styling, not everyone will recognize the about-to-be-famous bands and singers who added their considerable talent to The Bronze's ambiance. A few groups, such as Lotion, received a highly unusual, especially for television, five-second promo at the end of episodes featuring their sounds, but for the more acoustically challenged viewers, a quick musical round-up is in order!

1. **What traditionally becomes of a Gypsy's belongings after death?**

   A. They're buried with the body.

   B. They're cremated with the body.

   C. They're distributed among family and friends.

   D. They're destroyed by family and friends.

2. **Which *Buffy the Vampire Slayer* cast member played Jesus?**

   A. Anthony Stewart Head

   B. Armin Shimerman

   C. James Marsters

   D. Seth Green

3. **What television talk show host appeared in the *Buffy the Vampire Slayer* film?**

   A. Maury Povitch

   B. Geraldo Rivera

   C. Ricki Lake

   D. Rosie O'Donnell

4. **Who graduated from Ithaca College in New York?**

   A. Sarah Michelle Gellar

   B. Alyson Hannigan

   C. Charisma Carpenter

   D. David Boreanaz

## Who Was That?

**EPISODE PRODUCTION NUMBER: 5V17**

**ORIGINAL AIR DATE: FEBRUARY 24, 1998**

**WRITTEN BY: TY KING**

**DIRECTED BY: MICHAEL E. GERSHMAN**

### CAST

| | |
|---|---|
| Buffy Summers | Sarah Michelle Gellar |
| Xander Harris | Nicholas Brendon |
| Willow Rosenberg | Alyson Hannigan |
| Cordelia Chase | Charisma Carpenter |

### GUEST CAST

| | |
|---|---|
| Rupert Giles | Anthony Stewart Head |
| Angel | David Boreanaz |
| Mrs. Joyce Summers | Kristine Sutherland |
| Ms. Jenny Calendar | Robia La Morte |
| Spike | James Marsters |
| Drusilla | Juliet Landau |

For fans of Sprung Monkey, "Welcome to the Hellmouth" and "The Harvest" must have been like spinning both sides of a favorite record! No less than *five* songs from the group's first album, *Swirl,* enhanced *Buffy*'s premiere: "Believe," which the band performed during scenes at The Bronze, "Saturated," "Things Are Changing," "Right My Wrong," and, of course, the title track, "Swirl." Another of Sprung Monkey's tunes, "Reluctant Man," the sixth from the *Swirl* album, set much of the tone for "The Pack." Dashboard Prophets pulled the same double-header, being featured in the pre-

**5. What was the name of the Watcher played by Donald Sutherland in the *Buffy the Vampire Slayer* film?**

A. Martin
B. Merrick
C. Moulton
D. Mayo

**Jenny Calendar helped drag witchcraft—and Giles!—into the '90s, the *1990s* that is.**

miere and "The Pack," with three songs from their *Burning Out the Inside* album: "Ballad for Dead Friends" and "Wearing Me Down" in "The Harvest"; "All You Want" in "The Pack."

Succeeding episodes continued to feature up-and-coming acts.

Though many of the bands and singers featured musically also appeared to perform their work, lip-synching was sometimes a necessity. How else to have Dingoes Ate My Baby, Oz's fictional band, come up with Four Star Mary's rather significant contribution to the Buffyverse sound?

ANSWERS

1. D

2. A

3. C

4. D

5. B

## Everything I Ever Needed to Know, I Learned from *Buffy*

✝ Always get your key back after a breakup.

✝ Working late is never a good thing—
especially after dark in Sunnydale.

✝ Scarves and down-do's not only look great,
they hide tattoos, too!

✝ Having a guy draw pictures of you sleeping makes
you *très* conscious of your jammies.

✝ A librarian is probably not the best advocate to
discuss your sex life with your mother.

Christopher Beck isn't a name most music store patrons would immediately recognize, yet his influence is heard during almost every moment of *Buffy the Vampire Slayer,* a program noteworthy for its musical mixes. His eye on each scene leads to the haunting cello solos that underscore tragedy and the lilting quality of relief scored into the final scene of nearly every episode.

Also not to be forgotten are the minute-by-minute contributions of the show's own staff! Composers Shawn K. Clement and Sean W. Murray not only score the instrumentals that set mood and action throughout every episode, they're the creative couple behind songs such as "Anything" in the episode "Surprise," Part 1. Though performed by a professional singer, it was scored by Clement and Murray, who also oversaw its musical production. They're also the skilled hands—and ears—who handle the unexpected musical mix-ups that can't fail to accompany a complex production like *Buffy the Vampire Slayer.* When questions arose over the use of The Sisters of Mercy's "Never Land" in the episode "Lie to Me," Clement and Murray completely rescored the piece before it aired again within a few months. Only the first-ever airing of "Lie to Me" contains The Sisters of Mercy's version, but as with most things associated with *BTVS,* the quality never suffers!

# "Killed by Death"

the short version

J ust when it seems things can't get any worse, or Angelus any more sadistic, Buffy falls prey to an ordinary, if nasty, flu bug. With a fever heading towards meltdown, the Slayer can't walk straight, much less defend her loved ones and the rest of Sunnydale from a vampire with "issues" and delusions of grandeur. And, like everything else in Sunnydale, the hospital isn't what it appears. As if disease and pestilence weren't enough to occupy a bevy of doctors, Death himself is now walking the halls.

## Introducing Mr. Death

the longer look

*Heaven might be a wonderful place, but no one wants to die to get there!*

—*Jeff Moulton*

Try smashing yourself on the thumb with a hammer. Just try it. Give it the same knock-the-wind-from-your-lungs wallop you gave it a few years ago when you attempted to build that doghouse, or tree house, or bookshelf. Betcha can't.

(Well, if you can, you've got bigger problems than can be solved between the covers of *this* book.)

## Slayer-in-Training Trivia

### QUESTIONS

1. **Which of the following isn't a god of the dead?**

   A. Dis
   B. Hades
   C. Eos
   D. Pluto

2. **Who portrayed Buffy's father in the film version?**

   A. Dean Butler
   B. Ken Lerner
   C. Luke Perry
   D. James Paradise

3. **Who portrayed Buffy's mother in the film version?**

   A. Kristy Swanson
   B. Kristine Sutherland
   C. Natasha Wagner
   D. Candy Clark

4. **What do Jennifer Badger, Clay Barber, Sophia Crawford, Jeffrey Eith, Hannah Kozak, and Michelle Sebek have in common?**

   A. They're all stunt performers on *Buffy the Vampire Slayer.*
   B. They're all set designers on *Buffy the Vampire Slayer.*
   C. They're all script writers on *Buffy the Vampire Slayer.*
   D. They're all camera operators on *Buffy the Vampire Slayer.*

As Mr. Death discovers, slaying a Slayer ain't so easy.

Fact is, despite our incredibly thin skin, our pathetic unassisted land-speed records, and a tendency to run to fat after achieving the rank of coach-potato-with-a-TV-remote, human beings are gifted with surprisingly strong survival instincts. Bury us under slabs of earthquake-reorganized bridges, and at least one of us will crawl out twelve days later to have our picture taken with a sniffer dog. If one of our kids drops down a six-inch-wide hole in the ground, dozens of our species's adults will stop whatever they were doing to rescue the curious child. Kidnap one of us and an entire country will close up ranks against you. As Borghini, who lived to be 112, noted, "We spend nine parts of our lives coming up with ways to cheat Death of the other part!"

218

Death with a capital *D*.

While it's hardly startling that a show dabbling so freely with the landscape of our cultural consciousness would eventually focus on our universal fear of death, it *was* pleasantly surprising to see Death rendered as the vast majority of societies seem to prefer him—in person.

Hippocrates described death as an evil vapor, a "humor of the air rendering victims without the will to live." Even if he refused to follow the belief of his time, that death wasn't an elderly man striding through nightmares to claim victims with a clawlike hand, he couldn't escape his upbringing completely. His amorphous vapor, his "humor," continued to act with *intent,* to be actively in conflict with man. Perhaps we'd all like to think we're immortal, that only the intervention of some outside agency could cut short an otherwise unending stream of years, and that's why we stubbornly refuse to see death as the inevitable result of life.

Of course, *Buffy the Vampire Slayer* has always played with the definitions of *alive* and *dead,* throwing in the whole *un*dead kink to confuse the issue, introducing us to souls that can be evicted and retrieved with the assistance of some Gypsy chanting, a computer program, and a crystal ball. If we're to believe that Angel's soul is wandering the ether somewhere, it isn't such a stretch to believe that, somewhere, there's a doorman watching those souls travel back and forth, maybe even a doorman named Death.

Of all Sunnydale's denizens, Angel should be the most likely to accept that Mr. Death is wandering the halls of hospitals, jumping his unsuspecting victims, and sucking the life right out of them. With his Irish, two-hundred-year-old background, he'd have grown up with three of the best-known personifications of death—guess the Celts had a thing about death, too.

The Wild Hunt, a group of "people" that sallied forth from a different sort of Hellmouth to kidnap the living and drag them down to the underworld, appear in at least three different tales from Great Britain and Ireland. In Wales, the keening cry of a flock of wild geese heralds Death's imminent arrival and the impending doom of some leading member of the community. Also known as *Cwn Mamau* (The Hounds of the Mothers), the Wild Hunt

**5. Which of these classic vamp films isn't a pre–*Buffy the Vampire Slayer* spoof?**

A. *Abbott and Costello Meet Frankenstein*
B. *Love at First Bite*
C. *Once Bitten*
D. *Bram Stoker's Dracula*

ANSWERS

1. C

2. D

3. D

4. A

5. D

## Who Was That?

EPISODE PRODUCTION NUMBER: 5V18
ORIGINAL AIR DATE: MARCH 3, 1998
WRITTEN BY: ROB DES HOTEL AND DEAN BATALI
DIRECTED BY: DERAN SARAFIAN

### CAST

| | |
|---|---|
| Buffy Summers | Sarah Michelle Gellar |
| Xander Harris | Nicholas Brendon |
| Willow Rosenberg | Alyson Hannigan |
| Cordelia Chase | Charisma Carpenter |

### GUEST CAST

| | |
|---|---|
| Rupert Giles | Anthony Stewart Head |
| Angel | David Boreanaz |
| Mrs. Joyce Summers | Kristine Sutherland |
| Little Buffy | Mimi Paley |
| Ryan | Andrew Ducote |
| Celia | Denise Johnson |
| Der Kindestod | James Jude Courtney |
| Dr. Stanley Backer | Richard Herd |
| Security Guard | Willie Garson |
| Intern | Robert Munic |

appears as a pack of lean, white hunting dogs, who, with red eyes flashing and tongues dripping spittle everywhere, herd the souls of the dying towards the master, Death himself. It is he who ultimately sends them on the final path of their journey to the underworld. (Then again, anyone meeting an Irish wolfhound on a deserted road in the middle of the night might well figure the end was near anyway!) A slightly different twist to the story gives us the *Cwn Annwn,* an English version of the Wild Hunt in which ghostly hounds and the spirits of the dead race across the countryside gathering up whatever souls they can find in an attempt to buy their way back from the underworld in the only currency Death accepts.

While the Wild Hunt goes back to some of the earliest remnants of Brythonic myth, a more modern version entered Irish folktales just about the time Angel would have drawn his last breath. The Death Coach, which later turns up in French and Germanic fairy tales, probably owes as much to the increasingly more formal funeral corteges becoming common in even the smallest villages as to any religious or folkloric tradition. In the updated version, the person about to die hears the rattle of horses' feet and the jingle of dozens of tiny bells like those adorning harnesses. If the victim can see outside, he'll watch a long, dark coach, draped in black bunting, drawn by a three-horse team, proceed slowly to the front of his house. There's no driver apparent at first, no coachman on the seat to hold the reins, but in a short time, a door will swing open and Death's gloved hand will wave his victim to him.

The banshee would have been a quixotic creature by the time

---

## Everything I Ever Needed to Know, I Learned from *Buffy*

✝ Parents, take note: If your teenager starts *asking* to stay in the hospital, something really is wrong with her!

✝ Who says the flu can't kill you?

✝ Dividing all your acquaintances in "vampire" and "nonvampire" categories really simplifies your life.

✝ Chocolate covers all occasions that usually require a card.

✝ "Tact is just not saying true stuff. I'll pass."—Cordelia

Angel left Ireland. Usually female, the *Ban-Sidhe* (the Death Spirit) as opposed to *Leanan-Sidhe* (the Life Spirit), was never a common sight, even among the dying. She appeared to only a select grouping of families, those who'd been "touched by the fairies," a euphemism for those talented in the fields of music, or oratory, or literature. Even from them, she received mixed reviews. Descriptions ranging from a "young maid with spun gold hair" to "the Crone whose beaked mouth screamed" are all attributed to this same personification of death.

Beautiful or beastly, male or female, Death seems to walk Ireland's hills and shores in any number of guises, a trend that continues on around the globe. Buffy and her human-size compatriots

**Maybe if Buffy had frilly curtains on her windows, she wouldn't have been so afraid of the hospital.**

## Written on the Wall

**Though Buffy is back to her up-do hairstyles in this
episode, not a single shot is shown from the back! Guess
we still don't know if she finally got rid of that tattoo from
"The Dark Age"!**

\* \* \*

**Oops. When Buffy first peers into the children's ward,
there's no blue sign on the basement door, yet when we
come back to the same scene after the commercial break,
the sign is clearly visible.**

\* \* \*

**Okay, so we can't all be responsible for the continuity of
our dreams, but Buffy's dream sequence was way inconsistent. When she's first lying in bed, she's hooked to an IV,
but as she flips back the covers and gets up, her IV tubes
mysteriously disappear. Time is a bit mixed up, too. At the
beginning of the dream, the clock reads 2:27. The next
time we see the clock, it's 2:15!**

\* \* \*

could relate to Auraka, the All-Devouring, a huge Polynesian death
figure that "ate" his victims' souls after encasing them chest-high in
mud. Guta, a Hungarian demon, was into a little S&M before soul
stealing. He dragged his targets into dark caves, groves, or rooms
and then beat them to death, thus freeing a soul he could entrap. A
Lithuanian death figure, Giltine, followed Mr. Death's habit of
hanging out around hospitals. Traditionally dressed in shining
white, Giltine appeared as a beautiful young woman—but was visible only to those she was about to kill, usually by choking if about
to take a child and by suffocation if the victim was an adult.
Apparently, she kissed her male victims so thoroughly they couldn't
catch a single breath! Though several cultures depict death in ani-

malistic forms: crows, bats, owls, snakes, and the like, usually whatever was local and nocturnal, even these figures frequently could assume a human aspect if they chose.

The most modern death figure, recognizable by both North Americans and Europeans, and the most superficially similar to *Buffy*'s Mr. Death, is, of course, the Grim Reaper. Originally portrayed as a skeleton swathed in yards of black fabric, the Reaper carries a shining scythe, which we assume is handy in collecting the more recalcitrant souls on his nightly list. A British version of the 1920s, somewhat more dandified than the Halloweenish American symbol, depicts a fully fleshed man in an elegant but tattered morning coat and ascot, the very image of a down-at-the-heels undertaker with just a hint of the ghoulish in blackened eyes and gloved hands that just might cover less-fleshy fingers. Mr. Death with wardrobe quandaries!

Why would people from such differing backgrounds continuously portray their greatest enemy in their own image? Buffy knows the answer to that one. It's just so much easier to fantasize about kicking butt when there's an actual butt to kick!

EPISODE:

# "I Only Have Eyes for You"

the short version

Wandering the halls of Sunnydale High School becomes an exercise in survival tactics when a pair of ghosts start possessing anyone who walks over the spot where a student violently murdered his teacher who was also his lover. Floors open, wasps take up residence, and snakes run riot. As if to further blunt the Slayerettes' attempts to help Buffy exorcise the ghosts, Rupert Giles picks now to slip into an even deeper depression over the loss of his own lover, Jenny Calendar.

## What in Hell(mouth) *Was* That?!

the longer look

When the crew of *Buffy the Vampire Slayer* finally decided to do a ghost story, some thirty episodes into its schedule, they were clearly determined to honor the traditional tale, but as with all things Buffyish, they put a serious twist—or two, or three—into their version.

Sure, they included all the elements of a classic haunting. They had the "hotspot," a specific place—in addition to the Hellmouth's usual area of influence—to which this particular paranormal event was tied. (The fact that this hotspot was a dramatic balcony overlooking a steep stone stairway allowed for some stunning cinematography as well as a sharply defined

225

**Haunted? Yes. But by the wrong ghost.**

area of action.) They had not one but *two* violent deaths to serve as triggers for subsequent mystical happenings. This episode, building nicely on the events of "Passion," even had a third violent death to provide a red herring for a grieving Giles, though his stubborn adherence to the notion that Jenny Calendar was haunting the school does raise the question of why he would assume the woman he found dead in his bed *wasn't* killed in his house? How *did* Giles know Jenny was killed at the school?

Most importantly, "I Only Have Eyes for You" also had the repetitive behavior that defines hauntings. Just as the ghosts of two young boys are said to endlessly walk down the same set of steps at the Tower of London, repeating the same actions over and over, the ghosts infesting Sunnydale High were locked into a singular mode of expression. Everyone acting out the events of 1955 ran down the same path, spoke the same words, and ultimately came to the same end. Variation wasn't a highlight of James and Grace's reenactments.

Had the Buffy crew adhered strictly to the ghost-haunts-school scenario, there'd have been little room for the delightful plot twist that made an alternative ending—one that doesn't conclude with Angel and Buffy splattered over various walls—possible. Instead, they drew on two other paranormal phenomena to catch their audience—not to mention a confused librarian-cum-Watcher—off guard.

Your average run-of-the-mill ghost is actually sort of boring. It doesn't usually talk, or toss books about, or translocate every snake in the neighborhood to the cafeteria! Historically, it doesn't even say, "Boo!" No, to find something paranormal that actively toys with its victims, you have to turn to the poltergeist. If psychical researchers' accounts are to be believed, and let's face it, *Buffy* viewers are willing to suspend disbelief any number of times for a good story, poltergeists are much more "physical" in the human-relations field. They throw things, hide things, knock things over, slam drawers, and levitate everything from people to sofas to sewing needles to dentures!

In 1955 (pure coincidence on the date), Murray Seicher, a skeptical investigator from Raleigh, North Carolina, investigated a claim of poltergeist intervention at the home of Anna Weiser, forty-two, and her eighteen-year-old daughter, May. His reports, noteworthy for the sheer volume of incidents, some 812 over a nine-month period, include two events that would start that whole déjà vu thing going for the Slayerettes.

On June 16, Seicher wrote: "Strongly advised Mrs. Weiser and her daughter to vacate the premises today. In addition to recurrences of the loud banging in the south-east bedroom, Captain Weiser's display cabinets have become the subject of repeated, perhaps dangerous, incidents. Two pistols are missing from the left-hand cabinet this morning. Our attention was first drawn to these missing items by the discharge of a 1918 service piece inside the cabinet itself shortly after two o'clock last night. Being in the living room myself, I can state unequivocally that neither Mrs. Weiser nor May left the upper story until *after* the discharge, the hall stairway being in clear view from my position in the living room."

In the hours between the shot being fired and the household's normal start to the day, sometime around six-thirty, Murray Seicher prudently removed all live rounds from the deceased Captain Weiser's gun collection. He clearly recalls the presence of a pair of matched pistols in the left-hand cabinet. Though neither woman entered the room, the pistols were missing when he returned to lock up the cabinets. One was found three days later, lying in full view, on the front porch. Several delivery people and Mr. Seicher had passed the same spot during those three days and no one had noticed the presence of a gun. The second remained "lost" until early November when a cleaning crew hired to prepare the house for the Thanksgiving/Christmas season found it lodged under a heavy enamel sink in the basement.

# Who Was That?

**EPISODE PRODUCTION NUMBER: 5V19**

**ORIGINAL AIR DATE: APRIL 28, 1998**

**WRITTEN BY: MARTI NOXON**

**DIRECTED BY: JAMES WHITMORE JR.**

## CAST

| | |
|---|---|
| Buffy Summers | Sarah Michelle Gellar |
| Xander Harris | Nicholas Brendon |
| Willow Rosenberg | Alyson Hannigan |
| Cordelia Chase | Charisma Carpenter |
| Rupert Giles | Anthony Stewart Head |
| Angel | David Boreanaz |
| Spike | James Marsters |
| Drusilla | Juliet Landau |
| Principal Snyder | Armin Shimerman |

## GUEST CAST

| | |
|---|---|
| James Stanley | Christopher Gorham |
| Grace Newman | Meredith Salinger |
| Ms. Frank | Miriam Flynn |
| George | John Hawkes |
| Fighting Girl | Sarah Bibb |
| Fighting Boy | Brian Poth |
| '50s Girl 1 | Anna Coman-Hidy |
| '50s Girl 2 | Vanessa Bodnar |
| Policeman Bob | Brian Reddy |
| Mr. Miller | James Lurie |
| Ben | Ryan Taszreak |

On December 29, Seicher wrote: ". . . was forced to clear the house today. Despite the lateness of the season, a swarm of wasps appeared in the front bedroom during supper." Mr. Seicher, Ms. Weiser, May, and Margaret Snowden (a cook) were all in the dining room when they heard a harsh buzzing sound directly overhead. Anna Weiser was stung twice when she and Seicher went upstairs to investigate. A local volunteer–fire brigade records the incident as well. They were called in to use their longer ladders to reach the two second-story bedroom windows, which were forced open to allow the wasps to escape to the outside rather than into the rest of the house. Both of the firefighters who went up the ladders commented on how difficult it was to open the windows as they'd been painted shut quite some time earlier. A detailed examination of the room, the walls, the ceiling, and the attic space above failed to turn up any unknown nest the insects could have been using previously. Wanna bet the exterminators don't find any disturbed wasp nests in the attic of Sunnydale High School, either?

Though most people wouldn't think of paranormal investigation as a science of any kind, it does have its theoretical fads, and one of the latest poltergeist theories could cast a rather interesting light on "I Only Have Eyes for You." As early as 1889, investigators were commenting on how often a young woman was present when poltergeist-style activity was noted. In 1956, Claude Playfair put forward the notion that there was no "spirit" causing these bizarre incidents but, rather, it was a hitherto unknown psychokinetic ability being manifested by young women whose body chemistry was

## Everything I Ever Needed to Know, I Learned from *Buffy*

† The exchange of bullets is *not* part of a traditional courtship.

† If your school is forty-plus years old and it suddenly develops "automatic doors," be *very* afraid!

† Not even *two* days off from school makes up for snakebites.

### QUESTIONS

1. Which *Buffy the Vampire Slayer* guest star played two different characters in *The Addams Family* and its sequel, *Addams Family Values*?

   A. Elizabeth Anne Allen
   B. Bianca Lawson
   C. Susan Leslie
   D. Mercedes McNab

2. Which *Buffy the Vampire Slayer* regular left 'em rolling in the aisles as Frank-n-Furter in *The Rocky Horror Picture Show*?

   A. Armin Shimerman
   B. Anthony Stewart Head
   C. Seth Green
   D. James Marsters

3. Which of the following *isn't* a real hit song featuring vampires?

   A. "Dinner with Drac"
   B. "The Monster Mash"
   C. "Bela Lugosi's Dead"
   D. "I Gotta Wear Shades"

4. Which of the following films' plots feature characters forced to relive the same event over and over?

   A. *Groundhog Day*
   B. *The Lost Boys*
   C. *Speed*
   D. *I Know What You Did Last Summer*

## Written on the Wall

Oops. Historical flub. If the shooting occurred in 1955, how could the teacher and her young lover have been dancing to "I Only Have Eyes for You," which wasn't released even in demo form until 1958, and wasn't recorded by the Flamingos until 1959!

\* \* \*

Perhaps it was that thirty-second public service announcement directing viewers to suicide prevention agencies that made it more noticeable than usual, or the use of repeated footage (cast an eye over the two scenes of the Scooby Gang standing outside Sunnydale High watching the wasps, then start counting legs and see if you don't come up with two too many—Buffy's legs to be exact), but "I Only Have Eyes for You" probably felt shorter than other hour-long dramas you may have watched that week. Here's why:

## Breakdown for "I Only Have Eyes for You"

| ACTIVITY | START TIME | END TIME | TOTAL TIME |
|---|---|---|---|
| Teaser | 0:00 | 3:56 | 3:56 |
| Opening Credits | 3:56 | 4:45 | 0:49 |
| Act One | 4:55 | 14:04 | 9:09 |
| Act Two | 15:02 | 24:34 | 9:32 |
| Act Three | 26:48 | 37:01 | 10:13 |
| Act Four | 37:56 | 47:47 | 9:51 |
| Scenes from Next Week/ End Credits | 52:10 | 52:42 | 0:32 |

TOTAL ACTUAL EPISODE FOOTAGE: 42:41
COMMERCIAL/PROMOTIONAL TIME: 17:19

Barely two-thirds of the available airtime was devoted to the story line!

\* \* \*

> **THE FIRST SATURDAY IN NOVEMBER**
>
> "Whereas, there be inside our town limits a passel of gals what ain't married but craves something awful to be . . . we hereby proclaims and decrees . . . Saturday, November 4th, Sadie Hawkins Day, whereon a footrace will be held, the unmarried gals to chase the unmarried men and if they ketch them, the men by law must marry the gals and no two ways about it!"
>
> —Declaration of Sadie Hawkins Day, 1939, *Lil' Abner* comic strip
>
> \*   \*   \*

**5. Which film hasn't featured Sarah Michelle Gellar?**

    A. *I Know What You Did Last Summer*
    B. *Scream 2*
    C. *Buffy the Vampire Slayer*
    D. *Cruel Intentions*

changing rapidly. (The connection between hormones and the ability to shift large objects with your mind was never explained in great detail, however.) He speculated that the unresolved sexual angst suffered by these teens was being expressed through the "safety valve" of psychic energy. Playfair never claimed the young women were aware of their role in the "hauntings," just that they were the source of the activity.

Applying that poltergeist theory to this episode, we find a number of possible parallels. Anyone with more sexual angst than Buffy herself would be hard to imagine. Her mother is pissed. Her boyfriend slept with her and turned into a fanged fiend who likes to kill off her friends and her friends' lovers. She can't even get into a good no-holds-barred screaming match with her "ex" because, well, his soul has been evicted to another plane! Her presence might even explain some of the oddities in this particular plot line. Why forty-three years after the Sadie Hawkins Dance shooting? Why not fifty? Or twenty-five? Was it because there hadn't been a Sadie Hawkins dance in forty-three years, or was it because Buffy had just this year arrived in Sunnydale? Taking the numerous incidents as a whole, Buffy is the only person to have been present at every bizarre occurrence. She was there when Xander opened his

**ANSWERS**

1. D

2. B

3. D

4. A

5. C

locker, when her teacher took up "automatic writing" as a hobby, when Cordy received a plate of spaghetti in the cafeteria, and when she chose to take the hotspot as her part of the exorcism attempt. It was Buffy who dreamed of the ill-fated James and Grace, Buffy who heard James calling her, Buffy who observed the apparition of James in the music room, and Buffy who, as Cordy so clearly observed, overidentified with the ghostly couple. A psychical researcher could make a pretty good case for Buffy working out her emotional problems on a physical plane.

A straightforward haunting also doesn't explain why or how five different people and a vampire (who supposedly has his own extraneous spirit in residence) were forced to reenact the roles of Grace and James! Houses, towers, even bridges can be haunted, but the haunting of actual people is reserved for a whole different sort of experience called *possession,* a phenomenon that's already intrinsic to the entire mythology of *Buffy the Vampire Slayer.* Demonic possession is the cause of Buffyverse vampirism and the direct cause of Jenny Calendar's encounter with Eyghon. To include spirit possession for this episode isn't a great leap. It explains the forced mediumship of a teacher who suddenly takes up automatic writing and the actions of all those people who suddenly found themselves cast for the leads in a real tragedy.

While some purists might claim that combining these elements was something of a cheat, a way for writer and cast to make anything possible, the "anything" that it made possible was a new spin on perhaps the oldest of stories to be told around a campfire.

# EPISODE:
# "Go Fish"

**B**uffy starts sympathizing with bait when "sea monsters" take an unhealthy interest in Sunnydale's suddenly successful swim team. As the team's best swimmers are picked off one by one, and their coach begins acting as if he's about to win the Olympics, the Slayerettes start suspecting sea monsters are only part of the problem—and the school administration may be in on it!

the short version

## Who's Afraid of the Water?

Who's afraid of the water?

Well, and this is just a guess, nearly everyone if the water is deep, or dark, or reputed to be infested with monsters. If the water in question is deep, dark, *and* infested with monsters? Hey, Xander wouldn't be the only one "running like a woman," would he?

Man's fear of water's hidden depths, and the creatures that might lurk there, goes back to ancient times when a handy virgin was regularly chucked into the nearest deep lake to "appease" any gods, usually depicted as pretty horrendous monsters, who might live there. Our written history developed these fears into the *Here Be Dragons* warnings etched on the watery boundaries of medieval maps and the Nessie-type leg-

the longer look

233

## SLAYER-IN-TRAINING TRIVIA

### QUESTIONS

1. **What do Geoff Meed, Michiko Mishiwaki, and Eric Saiet have in common?**

    A. All three are script writers.

    B. All three played *Buffy the Vampire Slayer* vamps.

    C. All three received Emmy awards for their *Buffy the Vampire Slayer* roles.

    D. All three are related to Joss Whedon.

2. **Which of these watery films featured sea monsters?**

    A. *The Abyss*

    B. *Waterworld*

    C. *Jaws*

    D. *Creature from the Black Lagoon*

3. **Who was born February 20, 1954?**

    A. Kristine Sutherland

    B. Ken Lerner

    C. Armin Shimerman

    D. Anthony Stewart Head

**Sarah Michelle Gellar could've used some Buffy antics in her *I Know What You Did Last Summer* role!**

ends of more recent times. As film and television provided yet another way to record our collectively unconscious trepidations, the "creature feature" became a standard. While the cutting edge of the genre is as often determined by the latest special effects as by innovative writing, it remains popular by reaching deep into our psyches, pitting its images against the ones the audience itself can concoct. Some examples of the style, however, actually force us to not only enjoy our knee-jerk reactions but engage a few mental gears. Considering how well Joss Whedon and company play off of our other fears, it shouldn't be surprising that *Buffy the Vampire Slayer*'s "Go Fish" continues the tradition in a crisp, inventive fashion against the seemingly incongruous backdrop of a California high school—and makes no apology for playing up all the clichés and urban legends that surround the creature feature.

The very first scene in "Go Fish" probably made Sarah Michelle Gellar's fans go, "Hey, isn't that the same way *I Know What You Did Last Summer* started?" Sure, Gellar and her film costars played on the beach before starting their screamfest, but the setting is de rigueur for almost every creature-from-the-whatever flick. *Jaws* begins, as do Peter Benchley's other deep-water tales of terror, with bouncy, beautiful coeds toying with one another along the water's edge. The various incarnations of *The Creature from the Black*

*Lagoon* deviated rapidly after Act 1, Scene 1, but every single one began with the words FADE IN: EXT—WATER'S EDGE—NIGHT, and "As a young woman stares out across the dark water, small waves curl close to her toes." Sound familiar?

## Who Was That?

EPISODE PRODUCTION NUMBER: 5V20
ORIGINAL AIR DATE: MAY 5, 1998
WRITTEN BY: ELIN HAMPTON AND DAVID FURY
DIRECTED BY: DAVID SEMEL

### CAST

| | |
|---|---|
| Buffy Summers | Sarah Michelle Gellar |
| Xander Harris | Nicholas Brendon |
| Willow Rosenberg | Alyson Hannigan |
| Cordelia Chase | Charisma Carpenter |
| Rupert Giles | Anthony Stewart Head |
| Angel | David Boreanaz |
| Principal Snyder | Armin Shimerman |

### GUEST CAST

| | |
|---|---|
| Coach Marin | Charles Cyphers |
| Nurse Greenleigh | Conchata Ferrell |
| Cameron Walker | Jeremy Garrett |
| Gage Petronzi | Wentworth Miller |
| Dodd McAlvy | Jake Patellis |
| Sean | Shane West |
| Jonathan | Danny Strong |

4. Who hosted *Saturday Night Live* on January 17, 1998?

   A. Alyson Hannigan
   B. Juliet Landau
   C. Robia La Morte
   D. Sarah Michelle Gellar

5. Which actor played a priest on *Northern Exposure* before portraying a vampire on *Buffy the Vampire Slayer*?

   A. James Marsters
   B. Anthony Stewart Head
   C. David Boreanaz
   D. Ken Lerner

ANSWERS

1. B

2. D

3. D

4. D

5. A

**What every seventeen-year-old carries in her purse? Whatever happened to a lipstick and Dad's credit card?**

Beyond the first scene, story lines begin to diverge, but audiences and writers still find some small comfort in the universal constants, the touchstones that let both sides know just what sort of story they're participating in. See if you can pick out the same salient features in "Go Fish" that have figured in dozens of creature-feature horror films.

*The audience is meant to dislike, even hate, the first victim.*

They wouldn't want our first terrified reaction to their creation watered down by anything as soppy as sentiment. You don't think it was an accident that the first victim in "Go Fish" was the same guy who, just seconds before, was dunking the poor asthmatic's head up and down in the ice bucket, do you?

*The victims, preferably three in an hour-long format, will be perceived as progressively more sympathetic.*

236

Okay, so the second swimmer wasn't bobbing for brewskies with someone else's head, but do you actually remember him? Or, is it the third victim that sticks in your mind? Do you recall, with something approaching affection, his shy request to be walked home? Did his little wave from the swimming pool tug at your heartstrings? The writers certainly intended you to recall those incidents when Monster #3 started throwing our heroine against the wall!

*All underwater shots must be murky, jiggly, out-of-focus blurs.*

A whole beach full of clear water, and not one underwater scene. Stuff a school nurse or a buff Vampire Slayer in a sludge-ridden sewer and the camera dives into the action.

*It doesn't matter if the science doesn't work.*

Russian-fish DNA? Airborne steroids? 'Nuff said!

---

## Everything I Ever Needed to Know, I Learned from *Buffy*

† Anyone who thinks unlimited access to school-cafeteria food is a privilege needs to reexamine their priorities, not to mention their taste!

† Even the school nurse isn't safe in Sunnydale High!

† *Everyone* blames it on the Russians.

† Walk softly and carry a flutter board.
—The Swimmer-in-Speedos Credo

† Only in Willow's world do well-executed pie charts result in face-cracking smiles.

† Don't assume that haze hanging over the pool is just chlorine!

† If your boyfriend looks better with tartar sauce on him, get a new boyfriend!

† No coach should be *that* loved!

## Written on the Wall

This episode revealed all sorts of things from the hidden depths. Sure, we discovered there really are monsters in the sewers, but who knew that Cordy could draw or that Xander could swim? Wonder what Willow's hidden depth might entail? Rubber hoses and bright lights?

\* \* \*

*"Like an Oreo cookie, well, except for, you know, without the chocolaty cookie goodness."*

—*Willow*

Did ya know that, in one of her "child actress" moments, Alyson Hannigan was an Oreo-cookie spokesperson? Doesn't she just look like the milk-and-cookie type?

\* \* \*

Once again, killer continuity! Watch The Bronze's chalk-board! When they arrive at The Bronze, the board is blank, the standard set prop; when Buffy rushes out to find Angel, who is attempting to munch on Gage's neck, it reads *DJ 2NITE—NO COVER.*

\* \* \*

*Bigger is better.*

Ask Godzilla; size counts. Monsters, regardless of their source, are always bigger than their human counterparts, their human victims, or the humans hunting them.

Of course, recognizing these little similarities is never enough to protect us from the larger production, or to mask our instinctive fears. Carefully stroking our secret phobias and picking through our vague recollections of half-remembered "true stories," the best creature-feature writers know just what buttons to push. When the impossible happens, when a rare, startling incident draws mythical monsters into the real world, well, that just puts another tool on the writer's workbench!

Did the fact that the coach had a trapdoor directly above an open sewer, which probably broke dozens of health-code regulations, strike you as odd? What about the swim team's choice of party venue? If you had a whole beach to choose from, would you park your party at the end of a sewer pipe? For that matter, what's so intrinsically scary about a sewer in the first place? Sure it's gross, it's a sewer after all, but what would inspire terror? Plenty if you've ever flushed an unwanted goldfish down the drain!

Mythical monsters have been credited to the sewers of nearly every major city. In 1956, Chicagoans began flushing *before* sitting down after rumors of snakes finding their way up from the sewers began circulating. Frogs were the suspects in San Francisco and Detroit, but not just any frogs. According to witnesses, these were *giant* frogs! (Remember that Godzilla thing?) Just how a frog "as big as a dinner plate" managed to get up through a toilet's plumbing was never really explained. Intriguing as these reports were, though, it was the alligators in New York sewers—on the face of it an even more improbable claim!—that started the hysteria in other cities.

There really *were* giant alligators roaming around down there! There had been reports, of course; once someone even found a three-foot specimen in the Bronx river, but no one paid any attention to the gathering furor until years later when two New York City sewer workers claimed to have been chased from their work area by "monsters longer than a pipe length." At the time, a pipe length was twenty-five feet long! Teddy May, then superintendent of works, first denounced the men as drunkards, a claim they vehemently denied. Just as Buffy and Giles would find themselves knee-deep in scummy water as they searched for the truth of monsters in the sewers, Teddy May, armed only with a flashlight and a pair of hip-waders, descended into the depths seeking evidence of his decade's "sea monsters."

He emerged just a few hours later, shaking and distraught, with orders for wide-scale distribution of meat impregnated with potent poisons and a resolution to send armed guards along with any work party entering the sewers. May's program for extermination proved effective. The workers returned to their jobs unmolested. The panic faded away as larger issues such as World War II intervened. The particulars of the incident were filed away in newspaper morgues. However, the belief in huge sewer creatures—despite their existence never having been proven outside New York City—persisted to such a degree that, more than fifty years later, there's still someone who heard something, sometime, about something sort of similar. Not an archetypal memory by any stretch of the imagination, but certainly an inkling just waiting to be tantalized back to life in the mind of the viewer.

Regardless of how implausible the creature may seem to the casual viewer—and what exactly is *more* implausible than a DNA-stoked fish-steroid-mutant?—there's always the "equally strange things have been discovered!" When Jules Verne's tales of the *Nautilus* and its incredible voyages first appeared, reviewers applauded the creativity of the epic even as they snickered behind their hands at the passages devoted to the "giant octopus" and the mythical "kraken." Little did they know that *Octopus giganteus Verrill* and *Architeuthis*, a squid so large that it can leave sucker marks of more than a foot in diameter on the hide of a sperm whale, would emerge from the depths in less than fifty years! And, if those creatures aren't impressive enough, there's always the coelacanth, thought to be extinct for nearly 40 million years, but found living quietly off the African coast.

The allure of a creature feature isn't the science, the plodding explanations of how the impossible became real; it's the pure sensation of the ride prepared by a talented cast, a capable crew, and a script that upholds the traditions while still delivering the twist all audiences crave.

Besides, what exactly qualifies as "good science" in a program whose premise rests squarely on the supposition that vampires, the ultimate in creature-feature stars, actually exist?

# "Becoming" (Part 1)/ "The Whistler" (Part 2)

**B**ecoming" (Part 1): Buffy's suspicion that events are once again being manipulated by Sunnydale's three most prominent vampires gathers momentum when Kendra arrives back in town carrying a sword thought to be the only weapon that can be used against a stone demon—a stone demon who just happens to have also recently arrived and settled in at Sunnydale's museum. Buffy's suspicions firm up quickly when the demon is stolen, Giles is kidnapped, and Angel interrupts Buffy's final exams with an "immolation-o-gram."

"The Whistler" (Part 2): Alliances are broken and reformed in unforeseen ways when the Scooby Gang, separated by injury and circumstance, and the Vampire Triumvirate of Spike, Angel, and Drusilla, all find themselves working at cross purposes. Truly alone for the first time since arriving in Sunnydale, Buffy must make the most critical decision of her short life without the aid of prophecy or even Rupert's usual font of information and ethics pop quizzes.

## Surviving the Longest Months

*Buffy the Vampire Slayer* fans endured a brand-new experience during the summer of '98, an experience fans of other shows have come to regard as commonplace, if frustrating.

241

## SLAYER-IN-TRAINING TRIVIA

### QUESTIONS

1. Who actually filmed a part for the original movie but was left on the cutting room floor?

   A. David Boreanaz
   B. Anthony Stewart Head
   C. Seth Green
   D. Armin Shimerman

2. Who toured as a dancer with the artist formerly known as Prince?

   A. Charisma Carpenter
   B. Robia La Morte
   C. Sarah Michelle Gellar
   D. Bianca Lawson

3. What company's mascot goes "Grrr . . . Argh" and, occasionally, "I need a hug."

   A. The WB Television Network
   B. 20th Century Fox Film Corporation
   C. Mutant Enemy
   D. Kuzui Enterprises

4. Which actor did not appear in the film version of *Buffy the Vampire Slayer*?

   A. Luke Perry
   B. Rutger Hauer
   C. Paul Reubens
   D. River Phoenix

How could something so good-looking be so very, very bad?!

Reruns! Weeks and weeks of reruns! Because *BTVS* was a midseason replacement, its schedule had been a little off-kilter in comparison to other television offerings throughout its first year. The last episode of season one, "Prophecy Girl," didn't air until June 10, 1997, nearly a month later in the season than most other dramatic series, which wrap up during the early half of May sweeps. "When She Was Bad," the first episode of the second season, hit the air September 15, almost a month *ahead* of most season premieres, nearly *two* months before some shows such as the equally supernatural offering *The X-Files*. So, while X-Philes waited nearly six months for their obsession to return, Buffanatics faced withdrawal for only half that time—three months.

The summer of 1998 saw fans of *BTVS* casting about aimlessly for something to engage their interest between May 19, when the last episode of season two aired, and mid-October, when the next unseen episode was due to broadcast. It'd be a long five months.

However, Buffanatics are resourceful and imaginative. They came up with two games that allowed them to recycle old episodes in a new way. Perhaps you'll find them entertaining the next time you're complaining about the reruns that remain inevitable when modern-day filming schedules attempt to make twenty to twenty-four episodes stretch out over a year's fifty-two weeks.

## Buffy Surfing

The first game requires a considerable collection of scenes from *Buffy the Vampire Slayer*, and takes a little preparation time, but since the effort pays off with two variations of a single game, most fans are willing to put up with the inconvenience of figuring out how to use *two* VCRs.

Copy some of your favorite clips to a single tape. Short pieces with complete sentences work best, but make sure none of them have overtly obvious clues to tie them to a particular episode— unless you're playing the wimp version! Make sure *you* know exactly which episode the clips are from before you invite your buddies over (it's *so* embarrassing to be wrong when you're the referee) and make sure you have enough to last between an hour and an hour and a half. With a few bowls of chips 'n' dip, lots of sodas, two teams of friends who are as rabid as you are about *Buffy the Vampire Slayer*, and new batteries in the remote, you're ready!

The object is relatively simple: The first team to accurately recognize each clip gains one point (or a crack at the best dip if you find concrete rewards more motivational than abstractions like intangible points). The team to amass the most points wins—and buys pizza for the losers!

Of course, there are fans who find this basic version just too . . . well, too easy. They know every inch of footage, every glance, every stake thrust! No matter how short a glimpse they get, they'll nail the answer every time. For them, there's the "Quote It!" version. Remember our first bit of advice, short clips and full sen-

**5. On which soap opera did Sarah Michelle Gellar appear?**

A. *All My Children*
B. *Days of Our Lives*
C. *As The World Turns*
D. *Bold and the Beautiful*

ANSWERS

1. C

2. B

3. C

4. D

5. A

# Who Was That?

EPISODE PRODUCTION NUMBERS: PART 1, "BECOMING," 5V21

  PART 2, "THE WHISTLER," 5V22

ORIGINAL AIR DATES: PART 1, MAY 12, 1998

  PART 2, MAY 19, 1998

WRITTEN BY: JOSS WHEDON

DIRECTED BY: JOSS WHEDON

---

## CAST

| | |
|---|---|
| Buffy Summers | Sarah Michelle Gellar |
| Xander Harris | Nicholas Brendon |
| Willow Rosenberg | Alyson Hannigan |
| Cordelia Chase | Charisma Carpenter |
| Rupert Giles | Anthony Stewart Head |
| | |
| Angel (Angelus) | David Boreanaz |
| Oz | Seth Green |
| Mrs. Joyce Summers | Kristine Sutherland |
| Ms. Jenny Calendar | Robia La Morte |
| Spike | James Marsters |
| Drusilla | Juliet Landau |
| Principal Snyder | Armin Shimerman |

## GUEST CAST

| | |
|---|---|
| The Whistler | Max Perlich |

## PART 1 ONLY

| | |
|---|---|
| Kendra | Bianca Lawson |
| Darla | Julie Benz |

244

| | |
|---|---|
| Museum Curator | Jack McGee |
| Curator's Asst. | Richard Riehle |
| Gypsy Woman | Shannon Welles |
| Gypsy Man | Zitto Kazaan |
| Girl | Ginger Williams |
| Teacher | Nina Gervitz |
| **PART 2 ONLY** | |
| Detective | James G. MacDonald |
| Cop #1 | Susan Leslie |
| Cop #2 | Thomas G. Waites |

tences? Now's when the full sentences come into play. If you've had a sure touch on the Record and Pause buttons, each clip will present a single sound bite. It's up to your teams to come up with the next line of dialogue. Same rules apply, same rewards.

## The Unofficial *Buffy the Vampire Slayer* Drinking Game

There are as many versions of this game as there are fans, but the setup is pretty standard. Copy the list below, call up as many of your friends as will still watch *BTVS* with a fanatic like you, lay out an ample supply of either your favorite brew or a suitable nonalcoholic alternative. (My personal favorites are green gummy bears or yogurt-coated raisins, but animal crackers might be appropriate if you really want to get into the *Buffy* mood.)

If you're playing while watching a broadcast repeat, make sure everyone is comfortable, settled away, and provided with a copy of the list before the program begins. If you're playing while watching tapes, you might want to use two episodes and take a break in between, make an entire evening of your entertainment. In either case, make sure *you* have control of the remote. If you're the referee, you have to be able to settle disputes quickly. Just before you start, check to see that everyone's drink or bowl of gummy bears is within elbow-bending distance.

Turn off the lights. (It prevents people from sneaking an extra peek at the list!)

Now, play!

Take a single sip (or bite of animal cracker) when any of the following happen on-screen:

- **Buffy slays *something*.**

- **Xander wisecracks.**

- **Rupert Giles takes more than two full sentences to explain a simple concept.**

- **Angel says something cryptic.**

- **The library gets trashed.**

- **Giles puts his glasses on.**

- **Giles takes his glasses off.**

- **Willow says, "Wow!"**

- **A vampire bites someone.**

- **The Scooby Gang meets up in the library.**

- **Someone shows overt interest in some piece of jewelry.**

- **Someone says, "Hellmouth."**

- **Someone says, "Slayer."**

- **Someone says, "Sunnydale."**

- **Buffy sighs over Angel.**

- **Willow sighs over Xander, or Oz.**

- **Xander sighs over Buffy, or Cordelia.**

**And then there was one, again?**

- Buffy wears a cross pendant.

- Cordelia hands out unsolicited beauty tips.

- Principal Snyder threatens Buffy.

- Someone says, "Wiggins."

- Buffy shows a bra strap.

- Anybody kisses anybody.

- Buffy completely overwhelms Giles during a sparring match.

247

† Finals taken during a vampire immolation
shouldn't be held against you!

† There's no need to eat rat when you can steal
perfectly good entrails from the local butcher.

† Nothing good comes from kissing older women.

† Cleaning crews too lazy to clean between desks
aren't such a bad thing.

† Only *BTVS* could suggest murder and dating
aren't mutually exclusive activities.

† The vampire version of "take-out" doesn't include coleslaw.

† Every librarian-cum-Watcher should have
his very own Orb of Thesulah.

† Only in Xander's hands could fish sticks
become an educational aid.

† Being sucked into hell, or cramming for finals . . .
Not much of a choice there!

† Hugging can be a good camouflage technique
as well as sexually gratifying.

† A true love of the Manchester United football team just
might save the world—and they say football fans are violent!

† If you think bringing a college boy home to Mother might be
touchy, try bringing a vampire home for truly awkward!

† Rocks are good. Stakes are better. For sheer versatility,
you just can't beat a sword.

- **Buffy or one of the Slayerettes dances at The Bronze.**

- **Xander falls.**

- **A yellow happy face appears on-screen.**

- **A "WB" sticker appears in the background.**

- **Buffy has test anxiety.**

- **Xander shoots Cordelia down.**

- **Cordelia shoots Xander down.**

- **Something bad happens in the locker room.**

- **The Slayerettes hang around the graveyard waiting for someone to show up.**

- **Cordelia fixes her hair or her face.**

- **Oz drives a van.**

- **Oz says something really cool.**

- **Oz plays at The Bronze.**

- **Someone comes or goes through Buffy's bedroom window.**

- **We see the inside of someone's locker.**

- **Something bad happens in the cafeteria.**

- **Xander eats.**

- **The Scooby Gang is in the school after hours.**

- **Willow boots up a computer.**

- **Giles handles books.**

- **Someone performs a spell.**

## IN THE "WHY DIDN'T THEY—?" CATEGORY

Why didn't *someone* nail down those bookshelves after the earthquake, or the last attempt to open the Hellmouth, or after Ethan tried to dump the entire geography section on Buffy?!

Why didn't Buffy ever ask *her* Watcher for a stake of her very own? Although Kendra has had her wicked-looking implement long enough to name it, Buffy's stakes keep disappearing whenever she sticks them into a vamp! You'd think Giles would be man enough to demand a budget that went beyond disposable wood, wouldn't you?

Why didn't Xander, Buffy, Cordelia, or Willow warn Giles away from that museum? After their own field trips, the Scooby Gang *must* have known field trips only lead to *bad* things, right?

Why, in the several thousand miles of road between Manhattan and Los Angeles, didn't *some* cop pull Angel over for driving a car whose windows were spray-painted black?

Why, considering the fact they'd so carefully warded all their homes in "Passion," did the Scooby Gang pick the *library* as the location of a ritual they knew would be unpopular with all the local vampires? The same library that has been repeatedly invaded in a public building where one of the gang was already murdered?

\* \* \*

What is the vamp population of Sunnydale anyway? In just this episode, four "Anonymous Vampires" died, four more lived to help kidnap Giles, Angel was out chasing Buffy around the graveyard, and Spike was practicing his invalid routine. Eleven vampires. And we know there's more lurking in the bushes, right? "Five vampires in two nights," Xander tells us. Even if only those eleven "dined out" just twice a week, that's *1,144* unscheduled deaths per year! Not counting snacks and the odd death for some strange vampires-only ritual. They could empty a small town in less than twenty years!

* * *

Buffy kept hers under her spare stakes, but did you notice Angel's half of that pair of *claddagh* rings? Immediately after the events in "Innocence," Part 2, he began wearing it turned around in the opposite direction, a fact visible in several subsequent episodes.

* * *

Minor continuity blooper . . . What happened to Buffy's perky yellow hair buckle in the time between being approached by her L.A. Watcher and arriving back at her house a few hours later? Maybe she figured yellow wasn't the color for slaying vampires and redid her hair?

* * *

If Buffy's mother hadn't seen her up until the time the detective arrived at the Summers residence, where did Buffy ditch her shiny blue coat and come up with her dock-worker–street person garb? Does she have stashes of clothes hidden all over town?

* * *

What exactly was the point of using a choke hold on a vampire that supposedly has "no breath"? Why, to provide one of this episode's continuity errors, what else?

* * *

Catch the change in the Mutant Enemy signature scene at the end of "The Whistler" Part 2? Instead of its usual mumbled "Grrr-argh," it clearly says, "Oh, I need a hug!"

* * *

- **Buffy regales her mother with little white lies.**

- **Giles drinks a cup of something.**

- **Buffy calls Willow, "Wil."**

- **Joyce Summers mentions the art gallery.**

Have two sips or bites if any of these events occur:

- **A Slayerette slays something.**

- **Angel slays something.**

- **Buffy stakes something other than a vampire.**

- **Giles cleans his glasses.**

- **A vampire appears in vamp-face.**

- **Vampires invade the library.**

- **Anyone other than Giles speaks with an accent.**

- **Buffy says, "Oooh, knowledge."**

- **Someone mentions Los Angeles.**

- **Giles beats up anyone.**

These more rare incidents call for a healthy chug or gobble:

- **Anyone other than Buffy, Angel, or a Slayerette stakes anything.**

- **Giles's car backfires.**

- **A demon is identified by name.**

- **You actually know which band is playing at The Bronze.**

- **Principal Snyder fabricates an explanation for an unbelievable situation.**

- **Someone mentions or eats animal crackers.**

- **Anyone plays pool at The Bronze.**

- **Ethan Raynes turns up.**

- **Someone ends up naked.**

Drain the glass or polish off the bowl if:

- **Anyone comes back from the dead—and isn't a vampire!**

And raise your glass in silent reverence should Principal Flutie or poor Herbert be mentioned.

Obviously, this isn't the only list possible. When you get tired of this one, don't forget to make your own.

# Trivia Scorecard

You've watched every episode, pitted your skills against our trivia tests, and now it's time to see how you measure up as a Buffanatic!

125–150 You're *really* scary! You sure you aren't kicking for Rupert's job?

100–124 Willowesque, aren't we?

75–99 Probably wouldn't satisfy Principal Snyder, but Principal Flutie would certainly have approved!

50–74 Ah. Attempting to graduate from the Xander School of Lesser Cretins, are we?

25–49 Hey, come on! I bet Buffy does better on her finals than you did on this! Get thee to a library!

10–24 Perhaps you should keep a day job? Wouldn't want you stumbling into a vampire at night now, would we?

0–9 Duh!

# Photograph Credits

Page 2: Copyright WB Television Network/20th Century Fox/Courtesy Everett Collection.
Page 8: Bela Lugosi in *Dracula*, 1931. Copyright Universal Studios/Courtesy Everett Collection.
Page 13: Copyright Ngaire Genge, 1997.
Page 16: Copyright Peter and Ngaire Genge, 1998.
Page 20: Copyright WB Television Network/20th Century Fox/Courtesy Everett Collection.
Page 26: Copyright WB Television Network/20th Century Fox/Courtesy Everett Collection.
Page 30: Copyright Lorna and John Sainsbury, 1998.
Page 31: Copyright Lorna and John Sainsbury, 1998.
Page 34: Copyright WB Television Network/20th Century Fox/Courtesy Everett Collection.
Page 39: Copyright Peter Genge, 1998.
Page 42: Copyright WB Television Network/20th Century Fox/Courtesy Everett Collection.
Page 45: Copyright WB Television Network/20th Century Fox/Courtesy Everett Collection.
Page 47: Copyright Ngaire Genge, 1997.
Page 48: Copyright WB Television Network/20th Century Fox/Courtesy Everett Collection.
Page 52: Copyright Peter and Ngaire Genge, 1998.
Page 56: Copyright WB Television Network/20th Century Fox/Courtesy Everett Collection.
Page 60: Copyright WB Television Network/20th Century Fox/Courtesy Everett Collection.
Page 64: Copyright WB Television Network/20th Century Fox/Courtesy Everett Collection.
Page 68: Copyright Peter Genge, 1998.
Page 74: Copyright WB Television Network/20th Century Fox/Courtesy Everett Collection.
Page 82: Copyright WB Television Network/20th Century Fox/Courtesy Everett Collection.
Page 85: Copyright WB Television Network/20th Century Fox/Courtesy Everett Collection.
Page 88: Copyright WB Television Network/20th Century Fox/Courtesy Everett Collection.
Page 92: Copyright WB Television Network/20th Century Fox/Courtesy Everett Collection.
Page 102: Copyright WB Television Network/20th Century Fox/Courtesy Everett Collection.
Page 106: Copyright Universal Studios/Courtesy Everett Collection.
Page 110: Copyright WB Television Network/20th Century Fox/Courtesy Everett Collection.
Page 114: Copyright WB Television Network/20th Century Fox/Courtesy Everett Collection.
Page 116: Copyright WB Television Network/20th Century Fox/Courtesy Everett Collection.
Page 121: Copyright Ngaire Genge, 1997.
Page 124: Copyright WB Television Network/20th Century Fox/Courtesy Everett Collection.
Page 131: Copyright WB Television Network/20th Century Fox/Courtesy Everett Collection.
Page 133: Copyright Peter Genge, 1998.
Page 136: Copyright WB Television Network/20th Century Fox/Courtesy Everett Collection.
Page 140: Copyright Peter Genge, 1998.
Page 142: Copyright WB Television Network/20th Century Fox/Courtesy Everett Collection.
Page 146: Copyright WB Television Network/20th Century Fox/Courtesy Everett Collection.
Page 151: Copyright Peter and Ngaire Genge, 1998.
Page 154: Copyright WB Television Network/20th Century Fox/Courtesy Everett Collection.
Page 155 (top and middle): Copyright Ngaire Genge, 1996.
Page 155 (bottom): Copyright Steve Foster, Canada, 1996.
Page 158: Copyright American Broadcasting Corporation/Courtesy Everett Collection.
Page 171: Copyright WB Television Network/20th Century Fox/Courtesy Everett Collection.
Page 174: Copyright WB Television Network/20th Century Fox/Courtesy Everett Collection.
Page 179: Copyright Peter Genge, 1998.
Page 182: Copyright WB Television Network/20th Century Fox/Courtesy Everett Collection.
Page 187: Copyright WB Television Network/20th Century Fox/Courtesy Everett Collection.
Page 188: Copyright Peter and Ngaire Genge, 1998.
Page 192: Copyright Airborne Productions/Courtesy Everett Collection.
Page 196: Copyright Universal Studios/Courtesy Everett Collection.
Page 202: Copyright WB Television Network/20th Century Fox/Courtesy Everett Collection.
Page 206: Copyright Peter Genge, 1998.
Page 208: Copyright Peter Genge, 1998.
Page 210: Copyright WB Television Network/20th Century Fox/Courtesy Everett Collection.
Page 215: Copyright Peter and Ngaire Genge, 1998.
Page 218: Copyright WB Television Network/20th Century Fox/Courtesy Everett Collection.
Page 222: Copyright Lorna and John Sainsbury, 1998.
Page 226: Copyright WB Television Network/20th Century Fox/Courtesy Everett Collection.
Page 234: Copyright Sony Pictures/Courtesy Everett Collection.
Page 236: Copyright Ngaire and Peter Genge, 1998.
Page 242: Copyright WB Television Network/20th Century Fox/Courtesy Everett Collection.
Page 247: Copyright WB Television Network/20th Century Fox/Courtesy Everett Collection.